GOD
IS IN YOUR MESS

Your Crisis, Your Downfall

T. Gray

WESTBOW
PRESS®
A DIVISION OF THOMAS NELSON
& ZONDERVAN

WestBow Press books may be ordered through booksellers or by contacting:

WestBow Press
A Division of Thomas Nelson & Zondervan
1663 Liberty Drive
Bloomington, IN 47403
www.westbowpress.com
844-714-3454

ISBN: 978-1-6642-9684-8 (sc)
ISBN: 978-1-6642-9685-5 (e)

Library of Congress Control Number: 2023906270

Print information available on the last page.

WestBow Press rev. date: 06/05/2023

DEDICATION

This book is dedicated to the person battling their season; their crisis, their storm. I pray that God will allow my story; my testimony to offer you encouragement. May the words that flow across these pages speak to your spirit; reminding you that you are not alone, and that God is with you even in your mess.

ACKNOWLEDGMENTS

To my Father in Heaven, I say Thank You. There aren't enough words in the English vocabulary to describe how grateful I am to you. I had no idea at the time how I was going to do things; how I was going to make it, but YOU saw me through. There is no one greater than you. More and more I realize how much you love me. I cannot thank you enough; especially for this current season. This journey has been painful and thrilling at the same time. You are training me for the next level of my life; as only you can. I am proud to be your child. I love you with all my heart and being and I do not ever want to live one moment without you; I need you!

To my mom, this book is for you; proof of the belief you always had in me. The years you encouraged me to put my words out have now come into their harvest season. Thank you for believing in me. When I look back on my life you were there; cheering, supporting, and going to bat for me and mine. Thank you for the prayers you sent up on my behalf; God heard you and moved. I love you Momma; way more than you know!

To my dad, the one I joke and say is my true look alike twin. Thank you! The pep talks, and encouraging calls helped me through. Not to mention, the times you helped edit, talked through sentence structure, and grounded me when my world seemed to be spiraling out of control. I am grateful to have you in my world. I thank God for the relationship we have now. I love you!

To my real twin sister, my Best Friend; words cannot say how deep my love is for you. You loved me unconditionally and always cheered me on; even in the life- storms I cannot talk about. We have our own personal language that the world will never understand. It was priceless to me; the days you drove all the way across town to simply give me a hug when my world was raging. To me, there is no sister better than you God gave me the best. Thank you for always being in my corner. I love you.

To my beautiful daughter, thank you for being the wonderful person you are; always encouraging me and giving pep talks; like only you can. You are my biggest fan. For the many moments you assisted me with this book; even when I didn't want to hear any more about revisions, I cannot thank you enough; you were right. I am proud to be your mom and I love you.

To my handsome sons, I say thank you!!! I learned my most valuable lessons in communicating from you. Thank you for the many hugs you gave when my world seemed off. During the writing of this book; you listened, you cared, and it mattered to me. I am over the moon proud of you both. I love you dearly.

To my friends, thank you for all the calls to check on my progress, and to offer encouragement that the book will be good. I love you.

To my female support system; I say thank you for being my lifetime friends. God placed each of you in my world when he knew I needed you the most. I love you dearly. You will always hold a special place in my heart.

To Bishop, thanks for being a great friend; my buddy through school, and a positive male role model in my children's lives. You always believed in my writing abilities; I can't say thank you enough. May God always bless you and your family; you deserve it!

To my baby sister, thank you for helping me evolve into the woman I am today. I am grateful for the relationship we are building. Yes, I love you. (It's in print now, only you will understand.) You spoke things into my world without ever realizing it, but God knew what he was doing when he brought us back together. I'm glad you are my sister and my friend.

To the many friends and coworkers that have offered words of encouragement, checked on me, phoned, and gave pep talks during this journey; I say thank you! Your support in my book coming to fruition has been wonderful. I love you all.

To my past relationship partners, thank you for helping me grow. I was reluctant to write some chapters because we have all grown and are not where we used to be. Much love to you and many blessings. I wish you well.

To all the ministers, pastors, and church leaders both local and online; you all have no idea how much you have influenced my life. There are so many of you and the list is still growing. I am grateful that you allowed

God to move through you; never think that you don't matter. Being a vessel God uses; you are changing lives every day. Without us meeting, you have become like family to me; I say thank you! May God always cover you and keep you; your walk is NOT easy.

To my heart, my Handsome one; you know who you are. Thank you, Thank you! You saw the true me and helped me grow. Even in this moment, I have happy tears and memories of you. Thank you for pushing me to soar with the wings God gave me; that only you and God saw. You always encouraged, always believed, and then provided the tools (the laptop) to help me achieve this. Thanks for loving me and believing in me with the heart of God. You'll always hold a special place in my world! Every time I see the woods, a fishing pole, or a warm day in January; I'll remember you. In fact, if I were to get lost in the woods again, I'd hope it was with you. I miss you my friend!

CONTENTS

INTRODUCTION

God is with you in the middle of your mess, in your crisis, your downfall. This can be difficult sometimes for one to believe, but He is. It is hard to understand and comprehend that you are not alone, especially when that is exactly how you feel. It is also not by chance that you are reading this, or that I am writing it. Believe it or not, this is also a part of God's miraculous plan.

When you comprehend that God is with you, even in your predicament; not only with you, but will see you through it, life becomes easier to bear. Will there still be situations or crisis that come up when God is in your mess? Yes, there will be. I would be lying if I said there would not. However, sometimes half the battle is knowing that what you are going through is not a situation you must conquer alone, but to know there is someone with you who knows your strengths and weaknesses, who does not judge but welcomes you with open arms.

God is always there. Yes, I did say always. He cheers for you, picks you up, dusts you off and reassures you that you can do this, battle this, and conquer this. Not only can you overcome it, but you can soar. Afterall, God has all the answers.

It is like having your own personal cheat sheet for whatever life throws you. If you say to yourself, but my life is good, then just hold on; there will be somethings that happen in your life that in a split second, will knock the wind out of your sails, will trip you up, or dig you a hole so deep that you will feel like you can't get out of it. In other words, life will throw you some mess.

This is my testimony of God being with me in my muck. Everything that I am going to tell you happened to me and my family. Why, you may ask, did I decide to share this with you? Why, when I seemed to have been down and out, kicked and figuratively beaten, would I not give up? My response is…I understand where my blessings come from, and that the words I express about my life; may help another person survive theirs. I hope that you will read this with an open mind; knowing or learning how powerful God is. That He is the ultimate answer to it all.

More than that, I need you to understand that the same things He has done for me, He can and will do for you if only you believe. (Romans 2:11)

Let the words that flow across these pages, be an example of how to look for God in your storm… in your mess.

"For God does not show favoritism." (Romans 2:11NIV)

UNDERSTANDING YOUR MESS

ONE MAY PONDER OR QUESTION, CAN GOD REALLY BE IN MY MESS? I use the word "my," because as people, we have the tendency to personalize our situations. We may argue or question the fact that my dilemma is different than someone else's. As true as that sounds, the situation you are in is unique to you, but still a problem. It does not matter if your stuff is a troubled marriage, bad relationships, the loss of a job or a home foreclosure. It could be the repossession of a car, facing eviction, returned checks, or the fact your children are acting as if they have lost their minds. Not to mention, a health crisis of you or a loved one, drug addiction, being bullied or harassed, coming from an abusive home, or life as you know it is spiraling out of control.

Sometimes, your turmoil can also haunt you from the inside. The pain no one knows; like feeling unloved, grief, sexual abuse, molestation, physical abuse, and the hurt you simply cannot let go of. Realistically, any predicament that knocks you off your feet literally, figuratively, or mentally is a mess. As well as any confusion that hinders you from being the awesome individual that God designed you to be.

Occasionally, the pickle we find ourselves in; could really be you, yourself. Yes, I said it; you! Many times, we are our own foul-up. We belittle ourselves in our minds by putting our own selves down, telling us that no one wants us, or that we do not deserve this or that. If we are honest, we do not realize how often we will not even accept a simple compliment without interjecting a negative response.

It is hard to accept that every now and then; the reason life itself is in disarray is a result of you (yourself). In fact, it is going to have to be something deep within you that desires to get rid of your mayhem; for your situation to change. One must put forth the effort and work if they want life to be different. Look at this scripture or quote, *"I can do all things through Christ who strengthens me." (Philippians 4:13 KJV)* It does not say someone else's name, it says "I," meaning everyone can do ALL, not somethings, but All things. This includes every kind of mess there is. But how? I know your mind is questioning. The answer is there also; through Christ who will give you the strength and encouragement, which leads me back to this book.

Once you decide to do something about the pickle you have found yourself in and honestly you already have, because you are reading this book. You acknowledge that there is chaos, disarray or clutter in your life, and desire enough to rid yourself of it and search for answers; God will help you along the way.

Sometimes the how; is not for you to understand, just trust him with mustard seed faith that He will show you the way. A mustard seed is as big as the (.) at the end of this sentence. That is not much. (Matthew 17:20-21) All God needs you to do is take a step, no matter how small, in the direction of cleaning your mess, by seeking Him and trusting Him with the rest. (Isaiah 48:17)

> *"Because you have so little faith. Truly I tell you, if you have faith as small as a mustard seed, you can say to this mountain, 'Move from here to there,' and it will move. Nothing will be impossible for you." (Matthew 17:20-21NIV)*

> *This is what the Lord says- your Redeemer, the Holy One of Israel: "I am the Lord your God, who teaches you what is best for you, who directs you in the way you should go. (Isaiah 48:17 NIV)*

My testimony over the next few chapters, will show you much of the debris I have had, or found myself in, and the many ways God has shown up. Yes, I did say it, He showed up during my mess, my dirt, my pain. Did I see Him in the flesh? No, but still I knew, that I knew, that I knew, it was Him moving on my behalf. Hopefully, by the end of this book, you too will be able to see some areas He may have shown up in yours.

WHO AM I?

I AM EXCEEDINGLY, AND ABUNDANTLY BLESSED! WOW, WHAT A phrase but I am. This statement is personal, and an authentic belief of mine. The words are also lyrics to one of my favorite songs, *"Abundantly Blessed" by Ed Montgomery and The Abundant Life Cathedral Choir.* It is real; when you have an undying faith and belief in God, knowing that all things are possible to those who believe; (Mark 9:23) and I do.

> *"If you can?" said Jesus, "Everything is possible for one who believes.*
> *(Mark 9:23 NIV)*

My name is Theodora Gray. I am a twice divorced Mother of three beautiful children, Jolie, Ethan, and Solomon. My oldest two gifts were born during my first marriage that lasted almost six years. My third gift was conceived shortly after my first divorce; during a casual dating relationship.

Ever since I can remember, I wanted to be a mom and have children. I am not sure why I felt this way, but I did. Five children, five years apart was my plan. However, this plan was under the dream of a happy marriage and all my children with the same man; my husband. Being pregnant after a recent divorce and by someone I was casually dating did not fit my dream. At least, not how I had envisioned it. Yes, I would get my children, but not in a loving marriage.

Do not get me wrong, I had options, but during this period in life only one option was clear; to keep my baby. I had come to understand that God was in more control than I was, and that children are His gifts to us. In fact, there are people every day who desire to conceive children and cannot. As well as other people that will argue you down, they used every method of birth control to keep from getting pregnant and still got a baby. Therefore, I believe whole heartedly no baby exists without God putting his hand in it. This pregnancy was no different. Whether it was my plan or not; God's plan was for me to have this baby, therefore I was keeping it. Call it unusual but I also thought of my life expiring, and me having to come before God to explain why I chose not to accept His gift. I decided right there in that moment; it did not matter to me, who liked it, or not; because I realized at days end, I would be the only one standing before God, to explain my choice.

During this pregnancy, God and I grew extremely close. Later I married a second time, to an older gentleman, that had what I call HISTORY. Whatever history your mind can fathom, you are probably right. I share all this with you, so that you may understand, that I was not a perfect Christian; I had flaws and was flawed. I made bad choices and was in unhealthy relationships.

However, as disturbing as it may seem, sometimes one must go through some stuff, or find yourself in an unpleasant situation; to decide to make a change for the better. No matter what sort of confusion you find yourself in, no matter how terrible, nasty, or dirty that foul-up is, even how much there is of it; you can change it with God's help.

Look, I get it. If you think I am trying to convert a bunch of people into believing in a being; that right now they don't see or feel, well outright; that isn't my goal, but if through my story, you come to realize, that God is with you and can help you survive this hard game called life, then I have accomplished my goal, and ultimately God has too.

As you read, I am sure questions will surface like, how can she have this type of faith in God and have gone through so much? She says that He is in your crisis, but she found herself in tight spots multiple times. These types of questions can seem discouraging, but God had to allow my circumstances to be like yours; so, you can comprehend and relate.

Afterall, if I stood before you and always had money, always made the right choice, had a great marriage, never lost a job, you would not want to hear anything I have to say. However, when I tell you, I have not only had rough days, but rough years. Cars repossessed not one time, not two times, but multiple times. I have received eviction papers, been a magnet to the wrong man, lost a great paying job while my child was sick, been a single parent, raised my children without their fathers, audited by the IRS and more. I am like *Ellen DeGeneres* says in *her comedy show on Netflix*; I am *Relatable*.

GETTING OUT OF
YOUR MESS

I F YOU DESIRE FOR YOUR MESS TO IMPROVE, THERE ARE A FEW RULES to play by. The first and the easiest, is to invite God into your world. Yes, I told you that He is with you in your mess, and He is. However, God is a gentleman. He will not get involved unless it is your will. (Meaning, that you want Him to) God wants you to invite Him in your world, your heart, your life. He desires for you to seek Him, to ask for His assistance. (Luke 11:9-10)

> "So, I say to you: Ask and it will be given to you: seek and you will find; knock and the door will be opened to you. (Luke 11:9-10NIV)

The second rule is harder to do. Once we seek God's assistance, we must hand over the reins and allow Him to manage it. (Proverbs 3:5-6) So often we plead with God to get us out of our dilemma, or fix; only to end the prayer and figure out another way to get it done. God does not need you to tell Him how to do it. Afterall, if you had all the right answers, you would not be in this muck, would you? So, ask for His assistance and wait for instructions. He will give you a solution or strategy. (Psalm 32:8)

> Trust in the Lord with all your heart and lean not on your own understanding. In all your ways submit to him, and he will make your paths straight. (Proverbs 3:5-6 NIV)

> I will instruct you and teach you in the way you should go; I will counsel you with my loving eye on you. (Psalm 32:8 NIV)

Now, the solution can sometimes be a difficult pill to swallow but will always be for your good. For example, in my first marriage, during the dating stage, I pleaded and begged God to make Him mine. God had shown me the women troubles. I would dream their names, but I did not listen. The alcohol issue had also been revealed as it was a vital part of everyday life. Everything we did revolved around it, to the point that if we were attending a gathering where there would not be alcohol; he would try to get his drink on before we went or would make an excuse not to go.

God also designed each of us in His own image. (Genesis 1:27) We all have special qualities and characteristics that are unique and original, that make up who we are. God designs us not to be a carbon copy or shadow of someone else. We devalue ourselves when we lose our identities, by allowing someone to mistreat us. Mistreatment can be as simple as not accepting me for who I am, and seeing the uniqueness of my gifts, and as harsh as being physically, mentally, or verbally abusive, or allowing someone else to abuse.

So, God created mankind in his own image, in the
image of God he created them; male and female
he created them. (Genesis 1:27 NIV)

During my first marriage, I lost my identity. I had taken my vows seriously with special attention to the part, for better or for worse. In my mind, the vows did not say when life gets this bad you can leave, so I stayed. I grew up with a huge Christian background and we believed, what God has put together no man should separate (Matthew 19:4-6) So accepting the idea of divorce was not easy. However, I later learned if God does not approve of your marriage in the first place, then it is bound to fail. I could not be upset with anyone but myself, God had warned me, He had shown me the signs. By putting up with things, I lost me and who I was. I stopped loving me. Therefore, when I later asked God to fix my marriage, He did not. His solution was not what I wanted but, He did it for my good. Accepting this was hard, but deep down I knew it and understood that I deserved better, so I left. In leaving, I had to ask myself; why did I really put up with such foolishness?

Have not you read, "he replied," that at the beginning the
Creator made them male and female ⁵and said, for this
reason a man will leave his father and mother and be united

to his wife and the two will become one flesh. ⁶So, they are
no longer two, but one flesh. Therefore, what God has joined
together, let no one separate." (Matthew 19:4-6NIV)

If you cannot be honest with yourself, who can you be honest with. Afterall, everyone has skeletons in their closet that they do not want anyone to know about. No matter how close we say we are to our best friend, parent, sibling, or spouse, we do not ever become 100% transparent. Putting that sort of faith in someone else, to know the low down, dirty, dirty on us; Nah, I love you to death but, you will never know this; is how we feel, and it is ok. Realistically, I had to do an awkward thing and invite God in. I had to work on me. If life was to become better in my future, I had to look at my past. Looking back is not the goal. Never choose to stay in the past, but sometimes to know where you are going, you must first know where you have been. This can be extremely hard, because you must look at yourself under a magnifying glass and see your weaknesses and flaws. Not only see them but acknowledge them.

This means seeing the movie re-play in slow motion, pausing to say, man, I should have spoken up there. Boy, I do not like that! Another person does not need to know, but you yourself need to have what I call a come to Jesus' meeting and discuss your own short comings. Reveal to God the areas you struggle with and accept the times you had a hand in your mess. You must do this if you wish to grow and become better.

Maybe you do not manage your money well, and because of this you are constantly sweating eviction. On the other hand, maybe you are lazy and always late for work, and that is the reason you cannot keep a job. It could be you also, do not like to work at all. Whatever it is, get real with you. Realize that you are a work in progress and that God is not through with you yet.

For me, at the end of my marriage, I realized that I was so in love with the idea of being married, that I did not see that this person may not have been the best for me. Our lives were not equally yoked. (2 Corinthians 6:14). The things he wanted out of life was quite different than the things I wanted. It does not make him a bad person; it just means he was not right for me.

Do not be yoked together with unbelievers. For what do
righteousness and wickedness have in common? Or what
fellowship can light have with darkness? (2Corinthians 6:14NIV)

Even in my second marriage, I had to accept my part. I knew I was not interested in him; not like that. He was a good person with good qualities, but I was lonesome and afraid. The signs were there also. This was not good, if nothing more than the fact that I hid my marriage from my mom. If you must hide, dodge, cannot be real; then you are starting off in chaos. Add in his HISTORY, (that I am not going to cover here) and we have a huge mess; one I was quite aware of before I got married. Being desperate for companionship can cause a multitude of problems. Those prayers sent up to fix what you should not have been in from the beginning, are not going to go your way.

Sometimes God's No; although we do not see it at the time is the best thing He could have done. God is not a god of confusion but peace. (1Corinthians 14:33) If there is a lot going on, fighting, arguing, He is not going to turn it around, but instead lead you out of it.

For God is not a god of disorder but of peace- as in all congregations of the Lord's people. (1Corinthians 14:33NIV)

The third thing to do; in getting out of your mess is forgive yourself and others. Allow yourself to make mistakes and learn from them. Accept that you are not perfect and that there has been only one, that has walked the face of the earth that was perfect, and His name is Jesus.

Also know that your best - today will be different from your best -yesterday, as well as tomorrow. In other words, cut yourself a break. It is okay.

FORGIVENESS

A T THIS STAGE IN THE GAME, YOU PROBABLY THOUGHT WE WERE not going to discuss more on forgiveness, but we are. It deserves its own chapter and that is exactly what it is going to get.

Forgiveness is like a door that swings both ways. When one forgives another person, it unlocks the heart and allows one to become whole: let love in, have an inner peace. On the other hand, occasionally, the pain is too difficult to bear, so much so that forgiveness is off limits.

This type of heartache slams the door closed; breaking off the key in the lock. What is captured inside is infectious, fast growing, choking out kindness, laughter, and joy. People that carry this type of pain and will not forgive can be easily detected when you know the signs. What do you mean easily detected? Ask yourself this question, how many people do you know or have been around that are quick to lose their cool, yell and curse? How many people are never happy, always on edge, living for the next argument or fight? Do you know of any people that are extremely negative, quick to point fingers or identify someone else's short comings or flaws. (Hint: They often do this because someone has hurt them. They believe it is better to point out someone else's flaws, before someone sees mine). Ask yourself, if you know anyone that is easily annoyed because someone else is happy and doing well?

By now, you have thought of people that fit these questions. I know your mind is checking them off: the teacher, a co-worker; one or more of your friends. Even worse, someone close to you like a spouse or parent. They are sick and do not know it.

The pain has intertwined like a fast-growing weed, strangling the life and love from their being. Rarely do you hear them wholeheartedly laugh, rarely will they pay someone a compliment or have anything nice to say. They are the first ones to brag about telling someone off; never realizing, they- themselves are in pain. Whatever trauma or life event they hold onto has left them broken with invisible cracks in their foundation. There are even people wounded, and know it, but try to overcompensate by being the life of the party: overindulging in food, drink, drugs and often sex. Simply for lack of a better word, -broken. A broken person is so dangerous. Dangerous to others but more so to themselves.

Heartache affects the human spirit on many levels. Let us first access what the human spirit is. *It includes our intellect, emotions, fears, passions, and creativity (according to Wikipedia). It is also described as the mental functions of awareness, insight, understanding, judgement and other reasoning powers; according to models of Daniel A. Helminiak and Bernard Lonergan.* Add the word pain to any of those definitions and everything changes. For example, imagine a person in pain trying to use their intellect. Their ability to think, reason, or decide; all wrapped up in pain. What sort of decision do you think they would make? Not the best. Or combine pain and fear? *Oxford language describes fear as an unpleasant emotion caused by the belief that someone or something is dangerous; likely to cause pain.* Uh- oh, did I just write that? Yes, pain and fear equal the potential of pain, now we have pain causing pain. WOW! Have you ever thought of it this way?

Because you chose not to forgive someone who hurt you, you are choosing to do the same; inflicting pain onto someone else. The definition does not lie. Hurt people, hurt people. If you are still not convinced, please type in or google a book reference of hurt people, hurt people, and see how many books, all titled similar covering exactly that topic. *"Hurt People Hurt People authored by Sandra D. Wilson says just that, "When your pain causes you to hurt those you love."*

Notice it does not say the person who inflicted the pain but, the victim, who received it. Letting the pain remain causes there not to be enough room for the good stuff. If pain causes pain; then soon pain will take over, causing people to become hateful, angry, and bitter. Let us look closer. The person who caused the pain initially are no longer in the picture. They wreaked their havoc and left; vacated the premises, but they left behind the pain.

Now the pain sits down, it takes up residency in your heart and moves in all its luggage. Pain has a best friend named Anger and they rarely go anywhere without each other. Pain calls up Anger and invites him to hang out. Now these two are party animals and if they are going to do it, they are going to do it right. So, they call up their friends Devastation, Heartache and Bitterness who come in with a little liquor and some drugs. Boy, they are really going at it now; turning up as the young folks call it. But still the party is not there; so, Devastation calls up Sickness and she brings her two friends Anxiety and Depression. In no time the party has grown like an old *Faberge' Organics shampoo commercial; where she calls two friends to tell them about the shampoo and they call two friends and so on and so on, and so on.* The party is now completely out of control.

The heart has been consumed with nothing but the worst of things. It is no wonder hurt people, hurt other people. Their hearts have become sour like spoiled milk and rotten eggs. Love and hate cannot dwell in the same place. Learning to forgive is the only way to take your life back. You must take control of your life, instead of your life controlling you.

It is for this reason people say one must forgive, not for the other person's benefit, but for your own. When we choose to hold onto the pain, we allow that person to keep us in bondage to our hurt. They have gone on living their life and you are stuck in yours.

Forgiving sounds easy but it is not. However, it is doable. Sometimes there is physical abuse, sexual abuse, and other times mental. Physical and sexual abuse leaves detrimental wounds. This type of hurt is often unnoticeable to the naked eye and may leave damaging scars. Many people do not see the signs: your once loving daughter suddenly is bitter, snapping your head off, easy to irritate, her clothes have changed often for the worse; revealing and short. She seems to have checked out. In your mind, you write it off as if she is just being a teenager. There may be a comparable situation with your son; he no longer wishes to play the sport he loved, he is sassing off and talking back. You'd better start looking and asking questions because something has happened!!!

Many of you reading this know exactly what I mean because it happened to you. Please know that I feel your pain and I am so sorry. Even though this sort of pain is deep, you too must forgive, not for their sake, but for your own. Being real, it was not easy for me either, but I did.

In the same token, many people believe verbal abuse does not cause harm. However, I beg to differ. The old saying sticks and stones may break my bones, but words will never hurt me. That is a lie, a bold-faced lie. Rather than endure the harsh lashing of a tongue; you would prefer to have your behind beaten. A fist punch to the eye or a kick to the gut, one can heal from. You can heal from a nasty cut, broken limb, even a gunshot wound, but the re-occurring play back in the mind of harsh words filled with bitterness is horrible.

Psychologists say people ingrain positive and negative moments into their memory bank. *Rogers Thesaurus definition of ingrain is to implant so deeply as to make change impossible. Synonyms for ingrain are embed, lodge, or fasten.* This means verbal abuse, especially in women can become embedded to a person causing them to recall the moment over and over like a broken record. Ask anyone who has experienced this sort of pain and years later, with the same emotion; they will confirm the pain is still there, as if it just happened.

Now the thing is, the person that said it has gone on with their life never knowing the impact of their words on your being. If they had known, would they have wished they did not say it? Possibly? But we cannot dwell on that. Some people have no heart and would inflict more pain if they knew it; in this case it is best not to say. However, one must learn to heal. To restore, you must forgive. It does NOT mean you need to forget, only to forgive. You also do not have to become friends with them. Even the bible says, Forgive them for they know not what they do. (Luke 23:34)

Jesus said, "Father, forgive them, for they do not know what they are doing." And they divided up his clothes by casting lots. (Luke 23:34 NIV)

Words, words, words, whether it's' you will never be anything, you are going to be sorry like your Daddy, or even when you can think in a responsible manner then I will treat you that way. No matter the words or the combination of them used, they still hurt to the core.

So, how do we fix it? How do we heal from the pain? Again, I must say it is not going to be easy but, it is achievable. If the person that caused you pain was holding you down in a pinned to the floor fashion, you would fight with everything you have to get free; so free yourself from them by forgiving them. When you do, you take your life back. Love yourself enough to fight for you. You are the only one you have!

HOW TO FORGIVE

WELL, I APPLAUD YOU AND I THANK YOU FOR INVESTING IN YOU. The mere fact that you have decided to read this chapter; means you want freedom of forgiveness. Now there is not a straightforward approach to forgiving someone; so, I can only make suggestions. I can reference what worked for me.

God had revealed; during an attempt to find answers for a friend of mine, that there were things I was holding on to. In fact, there were situations I did not realize I was still carrying. As soon as the memory surfaced, the pain came flooding in. These things hurt me to my core, but I had finally decided to confront my pain.

I had a deep need to get away if I was going to tackle this hurt. I needed a space that no one would be watching. A place where I could be completely alone. I knew the filth that I had swept under the rug, dirt that would need to be exposed, sorted, and then permanently discarded for the last time. My solution was what I call a Me- vacation. I went on vacation alone; me, myself, and I. I found a decent hotel. I was not worried so much about the amenities, just that it was clean. When cleaning out your personal closet, you do not need a pool or valet parking. Simply a quiet space with no interruptions, a box of Kleenex and your method of venting. For me, writing is my safe- haven, my outlet; my way of dealing with life. I purchased a new notebook and fresh new ink pens. I also grabbed a bottle of wine, put on my comfortable pajamas, and got ready to work. I began with my first painful memory. I wrote the details down that I recalled and allowed all my emotions to come flooding in. I wrote down the names of the person or persons that caused the pain. It does not matter whether they recall the moment or acknowledge it. They are not important; only you. It was during this period; that I handed the incident over to God acknowledging that I must let this pain go, not for them but for me and to do so; I must forgive and leave it at Jesus feet. (1 Peter 5:7)

Cast all your anxiety on him because he cares for you. (1Peter 5:7NIV)

I found that letting it go was much easier than I had thought; as far as how I was feeling emotionally, and I was intrigued occasionally; at the years I had carried this burden. I am 52 years old and one incident which was my first recalled moment of pain; I was about 7 or 8. Think about the accumulation of time; at least 45 years that I had not let this go. Wow! To allow something to weigh you down; make you feel less than and keep you from living your best life for over 45 years. That is insane!

I worked each moment one at a time; often recalling things that I had forgotten. I did not stop until there were no moments left. When I finished, there was a great feeling of peace. As my friend encouragingly said, "I'm proud of you." "Those cleaning ladies have no idea what they disposed of on that day."

Do occasional memories come back or some of those people that caused the pain cross my path? Yes, they do, but it is my choice as to how they affect me, and I choose to leave it forgiven. Each moment I refuse to let the pain resurface, I feel empowered and in control.

Many people who motivate say, "It's not your ability to control the moment that makes you great, but how you respond to it."

There are options for forgiving a person and letting it go. Each process is different, and your approach needs to be what works for you. There is not a right or wrong way, but simply that you do. In some instances, one may need outside help in the form of a therapist, counselor or may even seek the church. Whatever your needs are; to help you become the best version of yourself, do it. You are so worth it.

*** **At the end of this chapter are scriptures as
well as sermons that can be accessed online,
to help with Forgiving and letting go.**

Now that we have a history of what mess is; we have a starting point of correcting it by letting God in. This is the key to being successful. Let's look at my life and see the many ways God has shown up. Please be mindful and aware that my circumstances are unique to me, but God is available to all, and He has no respect of person. The same as He has done for me, He can and will show up for you. (Acts 10: 34-35)

> *Then Peter began to speak: "I now realize how true it is that God does not show favoritism but accepts from every nation the one who fears him and does what is right." (ACTS 10:34-35NIV)*

This prayer was from a sermon: *When Past Hurts Still Hurt by Shawn Johnson*

Prayer for letting go of the hurt

God I'm ready. I'm ready to stop pretending, like pain in my past is not affecting my present. (Oh, this is so huge guys) *God, would you forgive me for holding on to unforgiveness, because I made all kinds of excuses and I got all kinds of reasons, but I want to get gut- level honest. I have held onto unforgiveness, and I got to repent* (right)*, please forgive me for holding on to unforgiveness today. I declare I'm getting rid of this unforgiveness and letting go of this hurt and anger. I completely forgive* _____ (put whoever you need to in there) *in Jesus' name because that's the only way I know how to go. I need the power of Jesus to do this one. I thank you that you are healing these wounds that were inflicted.* (You just pray that daily- your healing, your healing, you are healing) *you're healing the wounds that were inflicted and from the inside out, layer by layer.* (expect healing to come) *I thank you that you're making me whole and you're setting me free. I declare that I'm giving up my right to judge or punish. This person I completely forgive! It's in your hands now, in Jesus powerful name I pray. Amen.*

Sermons on Forgiving and Letting Go of Hurt:

T D Jakes: Making Peace with Your Past
Pastor Craig Groeschel: The Faith to Forgive- The Grudge
Joyce Meyers: How to Forgive and Let Go of Your Past
Pastor Steven Furtick: A Lesson in Letting Go

Joel Osteen: Drop It
Dr. Jamal Bryant: You're Gonna have to
PAY for what you did to ME
Michael Todd: Be Careful What You're Anchored To

Scriptures for Forgiveness and Letting Go

Ephesians 4:31-32	*Romans 12:19*	*Romans 12:17-21*	*Ephesians 4:32*
Romans 15:13	*Ephesians 4:26-27*	*Luke 6:37*	*1Peter 3:9*
1John 1:9	*Matthew 6:14-15*	*2Timothy 2:23-26*	*Luke 7:47*
Philippians4:6	*Hebrews 12:15*	*Mark 11:25*	*Philippians 4:7*
Luke 18:9-14	*Luke 17:4*	*Philippians 3:12-14*	*Matthew 18:21-35*

In all, there are over 50 scriptures that involve forgiveness and letting go. Apparently, God has every intention on us to forgive, and not hold grudges or harbor pain. In my own life, I had an awakening that even though I had forgiven the person; I was still harboring the wound; the hurt.

If you find that this happens, and it may. Go back to God and ask Him to sever the pain of the incident from your being, so you can heal. Notice I said, sever the pain, not the person. Not all relationships can or should be discarded, as we sometimes have been wounded by those we are in blood relationship with or a marriage. If you think you can't do this, think of Jesus and the sacrifice He made for our sins. He was innocent and He endured, so to forgive another, oh yeah- it can be done; with God's help. Free yourself and love you. You deserve it.

THE BENEFITS OF BEING
A CHILD OF GOD

THE BENEFITS??? BENEFITS ONE MAY WONDER, WHAT SORT OF benefits? Well, first for someone to love you un- conditionally is impressive! This means whether you get life right or wrong, God loves you the same. If you mess up; the marriage fails, you flunk out of college, you curse, have closet skeletons; no matter what, His love will remain. Even if you have accepted God and fall short of living (SIN) as we sometimes do; an example could be an addiction, an extra marital affair, you have abused, and He will still love you. Biological parents will walk away, and truly detach; but not God, He is still right there. If we speak to God, He is pleased to hear from us; if we do not, God is standing by waiting for the moment that we will.

He is omnipresent, meaning He is in our past, our current and our future. Because of this, God knows things from our earlier life that may cause problems in our future, and He takes the time to block, or correct those things. God also loves us enough to stand alongside when it is time to grow us; cheering like a parent from the sidelines, dusting you off if you fall short but, encouraging you: you can do this, get back in there and do it like I know you can.

He sits high and looks low. That means He has a full view of the course we are on. We can only see roughly 100ft in front of us but, God can see around the corner, down the street and over the next hill. He has a host of angels to be with you; every day, every step. They guard you like bodyguards; never leaving your side. That car accident, that you cannot explain why you did not get injured; that was Him. The bullet that injured but did not kill;

could have been deflected by an angel. Just like the doorbell that rang in the middle of the night to alert you that your home was on fire. It was all God or arranged by Him.

I know you may be thinking about the negatives that happen in life. If God knows all and sees all; why didn't He block this? First, you cannot prove He did not. There is so much He takes care of behind the scenes that we never knew of. Like the moment you wake up with a flat tire; it delays you, and once it's repaired or you catch a ride, only to find out there was a nasty accident on the highway. Did you ever think instead of being upset that you are late, that God saved you from being in that accident too?

The day you cannot find your car keys; although you always leave them in the same place. However, today the keys are not there. You search for 10 minutes before finding them. Now you are 10 minutes later leaving; only to find out the street you would have passed, had a drive by shooting during the 10 minutes you were searching for your keys. These things God does; blocking things you do not see. God also allows you to go through things, because it grows you, builds your character, and enlarges your territory.

Occasionally life moments will happen like losing a job and due to the loss, you begin the business that had been dormant in your Dream bank; never realizing the push was in God's plan. Upon termination, you became desperate. Desperate times call for desperate measures; so, you decide that you will give your business a try. Afterall, what have you got to lose? In no time you realize you are excelling. If you had not lost your job, you may have never tried.

God created the world and everything within. So, He has all the resources that you could need for life. You were created in God's image: unique and different, He knows what you like and dislike, how you love and desire to be loved, He knows the things you are great at and the areas you struggle with. Just like Toyota, knows what the Tundra pick-up truck can do; God knows what you are capable of; He designed you.

He knew you before you were born; (Jeremiah 1:5) and hand selected your parents so you would be able to fulfil your life's purpose. God parted the Red Sea, raised Lazarus from the dead, protected Daniel in the lion's den, and implanted a baby in a virgin. Not to mention, He did hundreds of other miracles. Don't you want Him in your corner, rooting for you?

*"Before, I formed you in the womb I knew you, before
you were born I set you apart; I appointed you as
prophet to the nations." (Jeremiah 1:5 NIV)*

Partnering yourself with Him is like having a Black American Express card with no limit. You have special privileges to do whatever in life. The benefits are too wonderful to name and to make sure we know all the advantages of what to do and not to do; he gave us a written handbook on living; the bible.

For example, the book of Proverbs is thirty-one chapters long; one chapter for each day of the month. If you read nothing but Proverbs; it will give you every aspect of living: what wisdom is and how it leads to a godly life, how to manage money, how to treat family, friends, parents, children, even coworkers. Proverbs warns of immoral behavior and who to watch out for, like the promiscuous woman. It speaks of controlling your tongue and reactions if you do not, as well as the keys to a great marriage; how to be the good husband, the virtuous wife. God thought so much of you, that He created a guidebook on survival. Yes, I would not want to live one day without Him; the rewards are too great.

A DUH MOMENT

I AM NOT SURE WHAT CAUSED ME IN LIFE TO NOT VALUE MYSELF better, but I did. At least looking back, I did not realize my worth. I started dating my first husband at the age of nineteen. There were qualities that were appealing to me about my husband although I was not immediately interested.

Over time, he convinced me to go out with him. We laughed, talked, and had chemistry. I enjoyed our time together, but he did not want a girlfriend and openly said so. He even indicated that he may date me and someone else. In my mind, I said okay, he is being honest and in the same breath; I desired to be his main girl. Just like he wished; we began as friends.

I understood the English language and comprehended what he said, but I knew he was interested in me and that I was different from the other girls. So, within a few months of seeing him, I would ask, "Do you think we could go from just friends to more?" he would say no. Then I would ask, "Do you think that we could then become better friends than just friends?" Once, we moved to that level, I would ask, "Do you think maybe, we could become great friends?" We took baby steps, or shall I say, he allowed me slow advancement. His favorite saying was "It is my world, your population." I thought that was wonderful, but thirty years later, it has a whole different meaning.

As we moved forward slowly; I would often ask God to make him mine. He had a beautiful personality, worked hard, but his weakness was the women. I saw all the signs. Even as we became closer, the women would show up.

I have always been very intuitive, so much so that sometimes it creeps the men out I have dated; especially my first husband. If he did something like dance with someone at a party; I would dream it and could even call the person's name. If he went somewhere and told me I am going here, but went there instead, when he returned, I would ask him, "So how was so and so?" He would ask me, "How did you know I saw them?" and I would respond, "I knew that's where you were going when you left."

Even with moments like this, I so desired to be the one he chose that I ignored what God was showing me. By the end of our first-year dating; he had given me a ring. I was over the moon excited and our wedding was set for two and a half years later.

I was strong in some areas and weak in others. He was honestly; honest. In our early days of dating, we had a conversation about marriage. He said he wanted to marry around the age of twenty-seven. At the time we were 19 and 21. I said, "Within the first year a person should know if the person they are dating is someone they wish to marry." "Any longer than that and they are wasting my time." That did not indicate that a marriage had to take place immediately, but you should know whether you want to keep this person in your world, for the long haul.

Even during the engagement period, I told him he was not ready to marry yet, but we did. To this day, I would say, he did honestly love me and even considered me valuable; valuable enough to not want to lose me, but not honest enough with himself to wait. My desperation for acceptance by a man showed I did not know my worth. He later said, when problems in the marriage arose; "I treated you the way I did, because you allowed it." Brutal words, but honest just the same. After many arguments and some physical fights, I officially called it quits in 1999; with our second child growing in my womb.

I moved back home with my mom until I could get my own place. One month and twenty-four days after leaving him; my husband, whom I loved dearly took our five-year-old daughter on a date with him to see another woman. I was devastated. It was exactly one week before our sixth-year wedding anniversary. Did he honestly think our daughter would not tell? There was also that possibility that he did not care if she did. Not thirty days later, I acquired a place of my own. I struggled but God blessed me with people that would help. My husband dated more and more; while I secretly prayed that God would save my marriage. Within a few months, he chose the other woman; and I promised her on that day she would never have to worry about me ever interfering in their relationship.

I am an attractive lady and it hurt bad that I was not the one he chose. Often, I found myself so filled with pain; that I could not find the words to pray. I knew God would get me through it and surprisingly I found comfort in the bible itself. At night, I would get my kids settled in their beds, and head to my room alone. With tears streaming, I would wrap the bible tightly in my arms and drift off to sleep. Never would I have imagined the bible itself would provide that sort of comfort, but I am grateful it did.

PRESCRIPTION FOR LIVING

O FTEN PEOPLE WILL ASK CHILDREN, WHAT DO YOU WANT TO BE when you grow up? My response would always be. "I wanted to be a wife and mom." I knew this early on. "I would add Architect and own my own construction agency, but primarily I wanted to be a mom."

At the age of nineteen, a gynecologist exam revealed: a cyst on my ovaries, fibroid tumors in my uterus and an irregular pap smear. The doctor stated he would keep me in my childbearing years as long as possible. My heart sank as I processed that my desire to be a mom was being threatened by these female complications. I asked the guy I was dating and later married, If the doctor said you only have X months to conceive, would he agree to help me have a baby? He said, "He would." A few years later we did marry and started trying to conceive immediately.

God blessed us in no time. We got married mid-March, and by the first Sunday in May I was pregnant. My pregnancy went well, and I passed the worrying stages of miscarrying as well as the stage of delivering too early. I never thought about the baby coming late. My daughter was born 10 days beyond the due date weighing 8 lbs. and 5 oz. She also had meconium in her lungs and stomach; which is the first tarry bowel movement a baby has. Doctors pumped the tainted fluid from her and a clear cake box device that circulated oxygen was then placed over her head to help her breathe and she was immediately taken to the Neonatal Intensive Care Unit (NICU).

This was a very trying time; as no one had informed us as to why she needed to remain in the NICU. I'm not sure if it was because I had run a low-grade fever during my delivery and got moved to a different floor. Either way, miscommunication left me uninformed. Finally, the day came, and I was being released from the hospital, but still had not held my baby. When the nurse arrived and began filling out my discharge paperwork; I was eating breakfast. She said, "At least you aren't like some moms and have to leave your baby here." I thought to myself, "Lady, do you not know that is exactly what I must do." She just kept talking and I did not say a word. It was all I could do to hold back the tears. No doctor had been in to tell me how my daughter was and being a new mom, I did not know what to do.

My husband noticed this upset me and when the nurse left, he said, "Honey, let's go see her." We went to the intensive care unit before leaving the hospital; scrubbed in and found our daughter. God placed an angel to care for her. The nurse saw us looking at Jolie and she walked over. Jolie was underneath the cake box with tubes and wires connected to her. She asked, "If I wanted to hold her?" I replied, "You mean I can?" as the tears began to flow. Confused, the nurse looked up and said, "Sure." I told her, "I felt Jolie would be alright, if I could just hold her." I explained that no one had told us why they were keeping her in the intensive care unit. Stunned, the nurse responded quickly, "First, I'm going to place her in your arms, and then I'm going to get a doctor to tell you why we are keeping her." God knew I needed that, and He put the right angel on duty. Just like the nurse said, my husband and I got to hold our daughter and the doctors told us they were doing a treatment of antibiotics because they had to pump her lungs and stomach.

I went to the hospital every day; sometimes three or four times a day to hold her and care for her. My heart had been extremely heavy with her being in the hospital this way but, again God moved. One day, during her time in the NICU my phone rang; it was my first cousin Darlene. She was asking how Jolie was doing? I am not sure what prompted her to say; whether she felt it or was just talking, but the next words out of her mouth soothed my soul. She said, "Jolie's going to be fine, remember I was born with a hole in my stomach and I'm still here." Those words reminded me, that God had cared for Darlene and would do the same for Jolie. Exactly ten days from her birth, we brought Jolie home.

Life seemed good for us, but in no time the warning signs God had shown before with the women and alcohol were back. Pictures surfaced and there were many fights; some even physical. His love of alcohol played a crucial factor. After many years of being disappointed, I had enough.

Five months pregnant with our second child and I said the magic words,

"God, I don't want to do this anymore." I let my husband know I was leaving. His response was "You will never make it one day without me." I told him, "If you think, I need you to make it, you have another thought coming; as long as my Father sits in Heaven, we will be alright."

At that moment, I had no idea the magnitude of my words. I had spoken into my future that we would make it. The power of the tongue. (Proverbs 18:21). My husband did not realize; he had given me a prescription for living. Each day that my feet hit the floor; I was determined to prove him wrong.

The tongue has power of life and death, and those who love it will eat its fruit. (Proverbs18:21NIV)

I cannot say it was easy raising my children by myself; it was not. We had rough days. However, it was not until years later of raising them alone that someone asked why I worked so hard. I told them, "Years ago, my ex-husband told me I would never make it one day without him and I was determined to prove him wrong." They asked, how long ago that had been? I said, "Years, because I had been pregnant with my son." They responded, "You're doing it!"

That was the first time I realized I was proving my ex-husband wrong. I often think of those words; now that my son is almost 24 years old. I had spoken my faith in God. At that point, my faith was mustard seed size but that is all I needed. My belief in God to get us through; never wavered.

In all reality, I never raised my children alone. God was always with me; right there in my mess. Because God was with us, we faired far greater than most. My children never went hungry; always had a roof over their heads and not just any roof, nice homes in nice neighborhoods. God looked out for us, and we were blessed.

Was I evicted from places? "Yes." Paying rent was always a struggle, but when evicted from one place, God always provided another. He blessed me with better jobs and a desire to hustle. I finally realized that my downfall was not a lack of ability to manage my money, but more along the principle of there simply was not enough. I stopped beating myself up for getting evicted and started producing ways to bring in more cash.

This resulted in a variety of businesses I have owned and operated. At one point, I remember filing taxes with four different businesses and a job.

Each of the businesses could have been great if I had focused only on one, but my mind was in survival mode. Survival mode meant this business income covered the lights, this experience paid the car note, this one helped with groceries. Being in this mindset provided me with different expertise that made money and blessed people with services they needed. It kept us afloat.

FORBIDDEN LOVE

THINGS WERE GETTING BETTER, AND I WAS FINDING MY WAY. I SOON met my youngest son's father. We worked together and although I was not paying attention to him like that, he was a humorous person to be around. Since my husband had chosen his lover over me; I often wondered if other men found me attractive. Would they be interested? I soon found out.

At that time, I personally did not desire a meaningful relationship. I needed time to heal; and my son's father had a baby momma. From what he said, they were not together, but were taking time apart to sort things out. So, in my world this was safe.

It was honestly a peaceful and enjoyable time to be in this sort of relationship with no real expectations. We laughed a lot, talked even more, and went out sometimes. Things were good for a while and then tapered off. There were lies told by him and the visits became less frequent. Then life happened, my menstrual cycle did not show up. I was like clockwork; I was never late. Even though, I had a female physical the week before and I had received a new prescription for birth control pills; I was pregnant.

Several weeks went by and I had not seen or heard from my to-be son's dad. I was approaching six weeks in my pregnancy; when my Monday – Thursday job announced they were closing. Days later my Friday- Sunday job gave notification that they were downsizing and relocating. How did you guess? The first shift to cut back was mine. What a mess!!! Here I was recently divorced and six weeks pregnant by a guy I was just casually dating who had become increasingly distant. I already had two other children aged 6 and 1 and now the two jobs I had; ironically both were going down the drain. Not to mention, family; close family, I thought would be there was not. How much more mess could I be in? Me and God became tight.

We became close more out of desperation on my part. In no time, I began to see that God was with me in my predicament. He promises that you are never alone and that He will never leave you or forsake you. (Joshua1:6)

> *No one will be able to stand against you all the days of your life. As I was with Moses, so I will be with you; I will never leave you nor forsake you. (Joshua 1:6NIV)*

My lack of mental support from close family members was deeply painful and caught me off guard, but not God. He knew this was going to happen and had planned accordingly. God knew I would need someone; not just someone in general but, someone who would always be there no matter what. A person I could tell the darkest secrets of myself to, and they would not turn me away. So, God blessed me with a twin sister.

I do have wonderful parents. My mom will go to the ends of the earth for her children and grandchildren, and I will do anything under the sun for her and my dad. However, the love of my sister, my twin is different. She is my absolute best friend, and she stepped in to help me through. During this time, God also placed three extraordinary women in my world to become lifelong companions.

He knew I would need them, and they would need me. Even twenty plus years later we are still friends. Our lives have grown in different directions but buddies just the same. No matter how much time goes by, one call from any of them will last for hours as we laugh and talk.

My to be son's dad dropped off the face of the earth during the pregnancy. Instead of focusing on the negative, I put my time into God and my children. When people would ask, "What are you going to do?" (Referring to my being pregnant and losing both of my jobs). I would respond, "I'm going on vacation."

I downsized from a more expensive home to one I could afford; to stretch my funds. I watched my spending and started enjoying life as best as I could. I wanted to be a better person and to someday become a good wife; so, I studied the book of Proverbs; with special focus on chapter 31 that describes a virtuous wife. I utilized the severance packages from my jobs to support my children and built my relationship with God, finding comfort in his word.

Each week, I would send in my tithes to the church and for the first time in my life, all my bills were current, and I was growing spiritually. I was not angry or bitter with my ex-husband or upset with the to be daddy. I spent time with my family and friends and even started writing. I began doing things I enjoyed: drawing, painting, baking, and sewing; things that made me, me.

I made it through the pregnancy and delivered a healthy baby. The dad completely vanished by the third month and has only had interactions twice between birth and 18 years old. I consider my son to be my gift from God; He just needed his dad to give him to me.

(Proverbs 31:10-31NIV) A Virtuous Wife

> [10] *A wife of noble character who can find?*
>   *She is worth far more than rubies.*
> [11] *Her husband has full confidence in her and lacks nothing of value.*
> [12] *She brings him good, not harm, all the days of her life.*
> [13] *She selects wool and flax and works with eager hands.*
> [14] *She is like the merchant ships, bringing her food from afar.*
> [15] *She gets up while it is still night, she provides food for her family*
>   *and portions for her female servants*
> [16] *She considers a field and buys it; out of her earnings she plants a*
>   *vineyard*
> [17] *She sets about her work vigorously; her arms are strong for her tasks*
> [18] *She sees that her trading is profitable, and her lamp does not go*
>   *out at night.*
> [19] *In her hands she holds the distaff and grasps the spindle with her*
>   *fingers.*
> [20] *She opens her arms to the poor and extends her hands to the needy.*
> [21] *When it snows, she has no fear for her household; for all of them*
>   *are clothed in scarlet.*
> [22] *She makes covering for her bed; she is clothed in fine linen and purple.*
> [23] *Her husband is respected at the city gate, where he takes his seat*
>   *among the elders of the land.*
> [24] *She makes linen garments and sells them and supplies the*
>   *merchants with sashes.*
> [25] *She is clothed with strength and dignity; she can laugh at the days*
>   *to come.*
> [26] *She speaks with wisdom, and faithful instruction is on her tongue.*

^{27} *She watches over the affairs of her household and does not eat the bread of idleness.*

^{28} *Her children arise and call her blessed; her husband also, and he praises her:*

^{29} *"Many women do noble things, but you surpass them all."*

^{30} *Charm is deceptive, and beauty is fleeting; but a woman who fears the Lord is to be praised.*

^{31} *Honor her for all that her hands have done, and let her works bring her praise at the city gate.*

IN THE DOGHOUSE AGAIN

I GOT OVER MY YOUNGEST CHILD'S FATHER AND DECIDED TO GO BACK to college as an older adult. Even though I was trying to better myself by going to school; my ex used it against me. We often had arguments over the children, and he would threaten to take them away from me every chance he could. I was a good mom: no drinking, no drugs, not out partying, but he still threatened. To help me de-stress; my dad and his girlfriend who lived about 45 minutes out of town offered for me to visit. I often did this to escape the chaos.

The ride was peaceful and quiet, as my children would frequently fall asleep in route. This allowed God and I time to talk. I was lonesome and the thought of raising the children alone frightened me. I often worried over how I was going to help my youngest child through life without a dad. Although my ex-husband and I argued, he was a decent Father. He also wanted nothing to do with the baby. One would have thought; I had gotten pregnant while we were married, and I had not. So, I knew for my son, there would not be a male around to teach him things; like my other children had.

During these visits to my dad's, I occasionally ran into his girlfriend's family. One of her brothers took interest in me. Although flattered, I told him I was not interested because he was too old; even though he seemed to be a good person. He would check out my car, do minor repairs, laugh, and joke with my kids. We chatted whenever I came to visit. Over and over, he would ask me out and I would respond the same way, "I don't see you like that."

Finally, I told him, "We can't date, but if you want to hang out sometime as friends; we can." I even told him, "If we are out and you see someone you are interested in, I have no problem stepping around the corner; while you get her number." One date led to a relationship and later a marriage. It was good at first until the big secret came out. He was addicted to crack- cocaine. A lifelong addict that had the ability to go for extended periods of time, showing no symptoms of abuse. Life went downhill and fast.

I tried to make things work. My vows said; for better or worse. They did not say, when life gets this bad, you can leave. So, I stayed. I felt if he hit rock bottom; he would quit, but realistically, if I stayed, he would never hit rock bottom. I was enabling him. He knew I would keep food in the house, lights on, the rent paid, there would be heat, and a place for him to lay his head. God was the only reason I did not lose my mind. God and I talked often, and there were days I would beg my husband to leave; just take your things and go. He had become verbally abusive, and I hated coming home.

One day the sirens went off in my head. What was I teaching my children if I stayed in the relationship? For my daughter, I was teaching her that it was okay to put up with mess. For my sons, I was teaching them that it is okay to be a sorry man, and a woman will still put up with you. Neither of these were good in my sight, and I started my plan to leave. Afterall, I did not need anyone to help me fail, I could do that all by myself.

Once I decided to leave; had made up my mind that I did not want to stay, God took over my mess. My husband's criminal history caught up with him and the police officers picked him up for a failure to appear in court and back child support. There was a large cash bond placed on his head and I had no money or desire to get him out. I did not know where I was going to go, but I surely was not going to stay there. I knew I could go home, but God had other plans.

It was like, once I decided enough was enough; God started moving on my behalf. I went through everything in the home and out of the home. I cleaned out the shed that was filled with all sorts of debris. Being married to my second husband was like being married to Fred Sandford of the television program Sandford & Son. Fred was a collector of junk, and my husband was too.

There was so much debris out at the road, that it caused the city collection team to send their supervisor out. The gentleman was nice and said, "If I would separate the junk, they would pick it all up." I had to put metal with metal, plastic with plastic, glass with glass and trash with trash. It was over fifty feet in length.

The more things I placed on the road; the more help arrived in the form of strangers. People would stop and ask if I was cleaning my building out and if I needed help in exchange for free items? I was thrilled. "Yes, yes," I responded. There were so many people, you would have thought I had hired a crew, but that's how God works.

WHAT IN THE WORLD....?

I HAVE BEEN A LONG-TIME HUSTLER; DETERMINED NOT TO FAIL. Afterall, my children were counting on me to keep food on the table and a roof over their heads. Over the years of raising my children; I have worked every kind of shift imaginable, been employed in a variety of jobs, and have gained a huge skillset for a female.

I was always willing to do a job that would bring in more cash, but it was even better when my children were small if it allowed them to go with me. A newspaper route became my source. After one night of training, I gained a whole new respect for the mail carrier and fellow newspaper carriers.

Most people never stop to think; that no matter what, the paper is outside, and the mail comes in the box. If there is a thunderstorm with lightning; they both arrive. If there are high winds like produced during a Hurricane; the paper and mail still arrive. If it is an ice storm or blizzard, although they may arrive much later than normal; they both are still delivered.

Until you drive a route, your mind never thinks of the conditions the carrier endures to provide this service. Imagine it is -2 degrees outside with a wind chill factor of -10 degrees. Yes, immediately you realize that is cold; not just cold, very cold and you do not want to be outside. If burr, is your instant feeling; imagine going outside layered up, getting in your car, turning your heat all the way up, and rolling your window down. Yes, I said, roll the windows down.

There is no way to drive and throw papers out the window or deliver mail with them up. Carriers will sit on one hand and drive with the other; trying to thaw out the recently exposed hand. To run my route, I would load my children in the backseat of my car; coats, car seats, toboggins and all. Then I would take comforters and completely cover them up; over their heads and run my route. Many times, they never knew, they had left home. I ran my route over three years.

It was early one morning, before the break of day and I was on my route alone. There is nothing more peaceful than to ride at night and see the world. Spiderwebs perfectly spun; coated in dew that glisten like jewels, deer and rabbits playing in the field, a thin cloud of fog hovering just above the dew coated grass, the stars twinkle bright against a black sky; it is a beauty to see and there is very little sound.

I had finished my route and was heading back into town; enjoying the quiet. In fact, the windows were still down as I relished the calmness of the day. I am not sure what possessed me at that time to fiddle with the radio. As I leaned forward to move the dial, I heard an odd noise; followed by shattering glass. Startled, I quickly turned my head towards the rear of my car; to see the entire back windshield was gone, with only glass fragments left covering the trunk.

Whatever it was had come through my open window and exited through the back glass. It missed me simply because I bent over to mess with the radio.

I have always heard God protects. If we only knew, as children of God, that angels are not only around us but travel with us; we would be amazed. (Psalms (91:11) They have saved my life or kept me from harm many times. Some of those moments I was aware of and there is no telling how often I was not. Thank you God, for keeping a hedge of protection around me and mine. (Psalm 91).

PSALM 91

[1] Whoever dwells in the shelter of the Most High,
will rest in the shadow of the Almighty.
[2] I will say of the Lord, "He is my refuge and my fortress, my God,
in whom I trust."
[3] Surely he will save you from the fowler's
snare and from the deadly pestilence.
[4] He will cover you with his feathers, and under his wings you will
find refuge; his faithfulness will be your shield and rampart.
[5] You will not fear the terror of night, nor
the arrow that flies by day,

6 nor the pestilence that stalks in the darkness,
nor the plaque that destroys at midday.
7 A thousand may fall at your side, ten thousand at
your right hand, but it will not come near you.
8 You will only observe with your eyes and
see the punishment of the wicked.
9 If you say, "The Lord is my refuge," and you
make the Most High your dwelling,
10 no harm will overtake you, no disaster will come near your tent.
11 For he will command his angels concerning
you to guard you in all your ways;
12 they will lift you up in their hands, do that you
will not strike your foot against a stone.
13 You will tread on the lion and the cobra; you
will trample the great lion and the serpent.
14 "Because he loves me," says the Lord, "I will rescue him;
I will protect him, for he acknowledges my name.
15 He will call on me, and I will answer him; I will be with
him in trouble, I will deliver him and honor him.
16 With long life I will satisfy him and show
him my salvation."(Psalm 91 NIV)

CLEANING OUT THE CAR

HAVE YOUR EVER HEARD A VOICE FROM WITHIN? YOUR EARS DID not hear it, but you know you heard a voice. No, I am not insane. If you are honest, although you may not openly admit it; you have.

It was early in the morning, my route was not complete when I heard a whisper; "You need to clean your car out; when you finish." I said, to myself, "man, I think I'll do it later." The voice said, "I said, clean out your car!" This time the voice was firmer in its tone, so I responded, "Okay."

Upon finishing my route, I reluctantly pulled up to the car wash and began the task of cleaning out the car. A newspaper carrier has in their vehicle left over papers, bad bags, banding straps, vacation sheets, copies of the route itself; not to mention other personal stuff. Because I had small children who were always dropping things in the car; I knew it would take a while.

There were French fries, empty cups, candy wrappers and other things. Once I got started, it was not so bad. I found myself doing a detailed cleaning; up under the seats, vacuuming under floor mats, and once in the front seat area, I pulled out the ashtray. Why would I think to pull out the ash tray when I did not smoke? There should have been no reason to look there for any debris. However, I understood immediately why God had instructed me to clean out my car. Within the metal ash tray, there was a glass crack pipe my husband had left when he drove the car. "That's what you wanted me to see," I said speaking back to the voice.

I knew my husband had an addiction to crack cocaine. Attempting to honor my vows of for better or worse; I had stayed in the marriage. I had warned my husband I would remain with him, but do not have it in my house, or around my kids. I also firmly said, "If I lose my kids behind you over some drugs; you'll never have to worry about dying from crack." "I'll kill you; because at that point I'll have nothing left to live for."

You may judge me for that statement, but I am human. I thank God I was never tested in that manner. I immediately went home and told my husband what I had found and instructed him to take everything he came with and leave. God had looked out for me and revealed what I did not know; protecting me once again. Thank you God for the whisper. (The holy spirit that lives within when you accept Christ into your life.) TD Jakes mentioned how the Holy Spirit moves on your behalf in a *sermon titled "The Holy Spirit-Your CIA agent (Part I and II)"* He could not have been more right!

UNUSUAL BLESSINGS

THE NIGHT WAS EXTREMELY COLD, AND I HAD JUST FINISHED SUPPER when the doorbell rang. A lady stood there, and she said she was there to repo my car. Over and over, I had fought this company with the payments. Most companies allow you to be behind for a couple of months before they repossess your vehicle, but this company was different. If your payment was due on the 5th of the month, they would try to pick it up on the sixth.

I had already dodged this company before; in a quick sweep by phoning my boss and asking if he could loan me my car note before pay day; three days away. He did and I reported that day to work late. I had gone to wire the payment. By the time I arrived at the job; the security guards said, "Two men had been there looking for me." They had sent the dogs, the repo people. Therefore, when this lady rang the bell; I told her let me get my coat and she could rest in her vehicle out of the winter air, while I removed my things.

My only car had just been repossessed but I was relieved. I would not have to stress any more whether they were going to pick it up. It is outlandish to think that after a while, the thing you have sweated over and worried about losing, when it finally gets gone, you are pleased. I had no car to drive but, I had a loving Grandfather who quickly gave me his older car that he was not driving.

I was thrilled and grateful. It was not anything fancy but, at this point, I did not need fancy. I needed four wheels that would take me from point A to point B. The car was old and did eventually start giving me minor problems. Had I known what I know now, I would have done some preventative maintenance things to help me out. With this car, I was able to work and be independent; not having to ask anyone for a ride. I called her Blue Bird.

Eventually Blue Bird started acting up and I was frustrated because that was my transportation and now, I was again without a vehicle. However, even when my car was not running, Ada's husband Ellis would bridge the gap.

Ada and I had worked together; and I noticed when we got off work at 3 am her husband would be outside to pick her up. At this time, I had great transportation and told her; he would never have to get out of bed to pick her up again. So, Ellis helped me with transportation the same way I had helped Ada.

My ex-husband would watch the children on the weekends when I worked. Although he had multiple cars in the yard; he did not loan me one or sell me one. One afternoon while picking up my children from their dad's home; his neighbor came by. He was a nice guy, but quite unique. He noticed that I was buckling my children in the backseat of my friend's car. He asked, "Where is your car?" I said, "The Hyundai was repossessed, and the car, Blue Bird was in the shop. He asked, "If my ex would loan me one of his?" and I told him "No, he would not." So, he said, to follow him; he knew someone that had an older car for sale. I did; and there sat Black Bird. The seats were dry rotting and I had to cover them with a bed sheet. The radio did not work but it was a car. I asked how much the lady wanted for it and he said, "I have already paid her; its' yours." One hundred dollars was the amount he had written the check for.

Wow, for the first time in my life; I had two vehicles. It may seem strange but, I considered myself blessed. Even though Blue Bird and Black Bird were breaking down all the time, I had reliable transportation. Never did they both break down at the same time. When I lost both of my jobs while being pregnant; I made a smart decision and purchased a newer van out of my severance wages. I had to make payments on the van but felt I could manage on my unemployment benefits. I paid my tithes every week and paid all my bills, cut corners, and guess what? I paid my van off with no job. This was the very first vehicle I ever paid off. Look at God, won't He do it.

SHAMROCK LANE

HAD RECENTLY FOUND OUT I WAS PREGNANT; FROM A CASUAL dating relationship, both my jobs were folding, and I decided I must make good choices for surviving the future. One of those choices was to downsize my home and try to find something cheaper to rent. I quickly found an apartment in the same complex as my sister-in-law. I applied and was approved; with a move in date of August the eleventh. My dilemma was I had to be out of the house on the 31st of July.

With this problem; I started to think of my options. I could possibly stay with someone; but I didn't really want to do that. I felt more confident in relying on God; people will sometimes let you down. (Psalm 118:8) My time was running out and desperation was setting in; when my thinking cap lit up. That apartment is not the only place to which I can move. With a simple prayer, I asked God to help me find another home and I set out to do just that.

I did not have much time, it was the 29th of July. I had only two days to move but, Gods' time is not like ours. (2Peter 3:8) He can work wonders in a few seconds if we trust Him. I knew that rental companies had leaflets of available properties that you could pick up from their outside boxes. I selected listings and started riding around to see where they were. I soon found a cute little two-bedroom cottage style house on Shamrock Lane that would fit my pockets. Now, the task was to get it.

It is better to take refuge in the Lord than to
trust in humans. (Psalm 118:8 NIV)

*But do not forget this one thing, dear friends: With
the Lord a day is like a thousand years, and a
thousand years are like a day. (2Peter 3:8NIV)*

I arrived the next morning at the rental company as soon as they opened. There was a nice lady in the office, and I told her I wanted to rent the home on Shamrock. She asked, "When do you need to move?" I told her, "Tomorrow." She looked up from what she was working on and said, "That probably would not be possible." "They could do a credit check that fast but, definitely not a background check." she said. I asked her if they would try. She assured me they would and asked if I did not mind; could I fill out my own application. She stated, "She normally does it, but was currently busy with a few things." I said, "Sure," and was glad, because this gave me the opportunity to pray over my application.

I quickly filled the paper out, laid my hands on it, and sent up a silent prayer, asking God to move quickly, that I needed to move by tomorrow and thanked him in advance. I turned the application in and paid the processing fee. I am not sure exactly what time it was when I left their office; other than early morning. I headed home to complete packing because either way, I had to be out by the 31st. I was thankful and I had a relaxed feeling. Even if I did not get approved; I had money and decided to stay in a hotel if necessary; before I would stay with someone.

Shortly after lunch, my phone rang; it was the rental company. The lady on the phone said "Ma'am, we have never had an application go through so fast." "You passed on the background check but, your credit is so-so." "Could you put down a larger deposit?" I informed her I sure could. She told me how much to bring and said I could come on and get the keys. Leave it to God. Time for God is not measured in our time. He can work it out.

MY GIFT

WHEN I MARRIED THE SECOND TIME, I MARRIED A GENTLEMAN much older than myself; 19 years to be exact. Although I was not really interested in dating him; we clicked and later married. He was a decent guy. He worked on cars and if his criminal history did not hinder him, he would hold down a job. One of the issues we often bumped heads on was his wisdom vs. mine. Because of the difference in our ages, our processing of thoughts was quite different. Occasionally, how he would ask you for something; ruffled my feathers. One day he asked if I was capable of going to the post office to get stamps. My response, I thought to myself, "I don't know if I am capable or not." (Duh, of course I can walk in or drive to the post office.) Why, didn't he simply say, "Can you go get some stamps?" It was clear; we did not always think the same.

We lived in an older house, and he came up with the idea that we were losing money by heating the house during the day when no one was home. I told him the house was too old and it would cost us a fortune to heat it up if we turned the heat off. He argued that it would not. Well, sometimes rather than argue; let's just see who is right. He decided since he was home working on cars, he would buy a kerosene heater, and right before the kids got home; he would light the heater to help warm up the house. For days we did this. He was good about getting the heater started early enough that the house was not cold. However, one afternoon as I pulled into the driveway with the kids; he was in a full-blown sprint across the yard. Smoke was rolling out of the back door. Although there was smoke, there was not any fire. The kerosene heater had malfunctioned; resulting in black soot everywhere. The soot covered everything. When I say everything, I mean everything: dishes, countertops, the floors, walls, bathtub, sink, table, and clothes. Everything! You know I was steaming, but sometimes, I told you so is not necessary.

We started cleaning. Soap and water took care of most of it, but the walls were different. When we started with the walls, the dampness of the cloth and the soot smeared. I told him to wait, "Let me go to the home improvement store and talk with the guys in the painting department." I said, "Let's see if they can tell us what to do." Once in the store, I met a knowledgeable man and he quickly explained that we needed to dry sweep as much of the dust down as possible and apply a thin coat of paint primer called Kilz. The skim coat of Kilz would be just enough to make the walls ready for painting. My husband and I both started together. He bought a paint gun to spray with and I bought a five-gallon bucket of Kilz. Afterall, the entire house needed to be treated.

The house was old and the modern amenities that people are buying today, to put in their homes called Shiplap was on the walls within. We began in the long "L" shaped hallway. With a brush, I began filling in all the little cracks and he sprayed. No matter how many times, I told him, we only need a light coat of the Kilz and then we would apply the paint color; he kept going over it repeatedly. Soon he said, "Honey, we need more Kilz." "What? "I said, really annoyed. He had used all five gallons in the hallway. That bucket should have completed 90% of the house. He asked, "How much the bucket had cost?" When I said, "Seventy-five dollars," he responded "Shoot, the next time, we better thin it with something." I told him, "Never mind, I will do it myself," murmuring under my breath, I told you…

I would paint a little at a time, room by room and I soon realized that I loved to paint. I would select my colors, put on my music, and watch the transformation take place. I was very particular about how I wanted it to look. After painting my own home, one of my friends asked me to help paint their rental house. I told her I would, if no one else painted in the room I was working in.

Years later, coworkers and I got to talking about painting. I told them that I loved to paint and one of the guys said, "If you really like to paint like that, I have rental property." "Come give me an estimate and I will give you a try." I said sure, not knowing anything about creating an estimate. I shot myself in the foot by charging only (do not laugh) $450 to paint three bedrooms, one bath, the kitchen, cabinets, trim, molding, and doors.

I worked and worked and did an excellent job. After that, he would call every time he had a unit come open. I gained more painting experience and started thinking of ways to cut down on time. It was like I had been born with the concept of painting. I started a technique I called cutting in, to save time on taping off everything, not realizing the professional painters call it cutting in. God had placed painting in my DNA.

In no time, I was getting more painting jobs and I now own a painting business that operates by word of mouth only and have been in operation for over eleven years. The business really leaped when my son got sick and combined with cleaning saved my neck. This girl due to a foul-up with a malfunctioning kerosene heater discovered one of her gifts.

Every person is born with a seed/ gift inside of them. *A gift opens the way and ushers the giver into the presence of the great. (Proverbs 18:16NIV)* In other words, your gift will make room for you. *Martin Luther King Jr. quoted Ralph Waldo Emerson, the great essayist in a lecture in 1871. "If a man can write a better book, preach a better sermon or make a better mousetrap than his neighbor, even if he builds his house in the woods, the world will make a beaten path to his door."* The speech was *"What is Your Life's Blueprint?"*

I challenge you my friend; to find your gift. Your life's blueprint. Hint: You were born with it. It is already within you, so rather than find it, ask God to develop it. It will make room for you, like mine has made for me.

WHEN GOD IS UP TO SOMETHING

MY HUSBAND HAD BEEN ARRESTED ON WARRANT CHARGES, AND I was packing up to move. After getting all the junk out, I meticulously cleaned and packed up the inner contents of the home. I purchased totes, washed up all my husband's things, and neatly packed them away. His tools I packed up too and arranged for them to be delivered to him as soon as he was released.

While preparing for our future move somewhere; my friend Farrah called needing my help. Farrah ran a cleaning service and over the years I often assisted her. "Can you cover a customer today?" "Sure," I said. When I arrived at the lady's home, I apologized for running late; explaining that I had been looking for a house to rent. She quickly said, "No problem, Farrah had said you were trying to move." She went on to say she had rental property and asked what I could afford. I told her and she said, "When you leave take this key and look at this house." "It is yours, if you want it." I was surprised but was sure from the address that I was not going to take it.

In my mind, I tried to be hopeful, but was correct about its location. The house was nice, but the neighborhood not so much. I returned the key and told her politely, "I really appreciate the offer and that the house is nice, but my children are small, and I don't want to have to worry about whether someone is going to try and rob me; while I am taking them in or out of the car." "Thank you, but I cannot take it."

Days later, my friend Farrah called again and said the same lady was trying to contact me. "For what," I asked. She said, "Her father has two houses, both share a driveway; he knows your situation and he said, you can pick which one you want. They are both empty." Again, I was shocked.

I went to look at the houses and found them to be beautiful and newly built; within the last two years. I quickly called the lady back and asked how much? She said, "He rents them for $900, but knows you can't afford that and will bring it down to the amount you can pay. I told her okay but explained that I did not currently have any money to move with and would not have any until the first of the month. His response, "I know that, but you have got to have somewhere to go now, so pick one and I will send over the keys." "The water and lights are already on and the one in the back has all the appliances." he said. The houses were in an older neighborhood, in a safe place, and on the better side of town; not easy for my ex-husband to find. So, I chose the one farthest off the road.

When I walked into the house; tears began to roll down my face. God had given me not just any house, but a new house; with three bedrooms, two full baths, a laundry room that came with a washer and a dryer, a huge kitchen with stove, refrigerator, dishwasher, and microwave, Berber carpeting, a fireplace, front porch, and a deck on the back. God did it!!! He blessed me with a home; a safe- haven for me and my children. It was as if God had said, I was waiting for you to remove the un-necessary stuff in your world, so that I could bless you.

My blessings began in an overwhelming way; however, all things were not peaches and cream. I struggled financially but saw more of how God was moving in my life and on my behalf.

Please do not mistake what I am saying; as we lightly struggled. I had cars, noticed I did not say a car, but more than one car repossessed. I got in trouble with the property owner on my rent. I rode dirty at times with expired tags and un-insured vehicles. I wrote bad checks as a way of stalling for things and would pay for the extra insufficient fees. There were often overdrawn bank accounts, some of them even closed due to negative balances. Now, do not get me wrong, I did not bounce checks to go shopping, buying clothes or shoes, but I would write a bad check to keep the lights on or buy groceries. It is not something that I am proud of, but it happened. Thank you, Jesus, God will not let you look like what you have been through.

GOD KNOWS MY NAME

I T WAS MID- NOVEMBER 2007, AND PEOPLE WERE OUT SHOPPING FOR Christmas. The company that I worked for; teamed up with the local television station to promote Toys for Kids.

This Toys for Kids program had been in effect for years and was set up to raise gifts for children that are less fortunate. They tried to make sure no child would be without for Christmas. Through advertisement over the airways and our stores; there was a daily abundance of toys coming through: bicycles, baby dolls, remote control cars, games, bakeware sets, and tools.

This particular year, it was my assignment to coordinate all the stores in the campaign. I was eager to help and always tried to make sure my children had gifts for Christmas; as well as any other child, if I had my way. Because of this, I created additional ways to collect extra money for our store. We had a cash donation location at the drop off spot for the toys, but I thought of a way to collect loose change at the register. I designed glass jars decorated nicely for Christmas with lids, and a sign indicating what it was for. Each day I would make sure the jars were set out and retrieved at closing time; forwarding all funds to the appropriate person. With the monetary donations, teams of people would go to the local toy stores and shop for the children.

I did not have much money, but I also did not want any child to get up on Christmas and not have a gift. Every pay day, I would purchase a small toy or something in my price range to add to the bin. My money was always short for Christmas, but I always managed to give gifts to my kids. I would often do last-minute shopping, but this was the month of November, and I was not thinking from a selfish point of view.

One afternoon my children's elementary school called; I thought something was wrong. It was the principal on the line. "Every year she said, the teachers would sponsor a family for Christmas and your family was selected." She said, "We would like to bring the items by before Christmas, this way you can say it's from you." I told her "Thank you, thank you, but I would not say the gifts were from me." "When blessings come in, I tell the children look how God works and I will tell them how we got this blessing too." Upon arriving at my home, tears streamed. There were bicycles, shoes, and clothing items. The same Christmas, I received another phone call from the Girl Scout Troop Leader; her church had also adopted us for Christmas. There were gift cards for food and shopping. Even to this day, when I think about my name coming up to people who did not know me; for them to bless us, only God, only God!

I understood from early in life that God knew my name. He created me, but realizing that (for lack of a better word) ... For real, for real; that He is this close to me, He is watching and waiting, and He is moving and shaking on my behalf. For Him to whisper to someone; what about Theodora's family? These people did not know me. Someone who knew me, spoke of me to someone else to bless me. Although other people's names were submitted for the gifts, I was the one chosen; nothing but God!!!

HE WORKED IT OUT!

ONE DAY WHILE LIVING ON SHAMROCK LANE, I RECEIVED AN advertising mailer promoting Massage Classes at the local community college. I called about the classes. After checking the cost, I did not enroll but, the next semester inquired again. At the time the classes were to start I still could not go. Each time I received a new flyer, I would ask again. Years later while working one night unloading trucks, co-workers and I got to talking about what we would go back to school for, if given the opportunity. I stated I would love to take Massage Therapy. A coworker of mine said, "For real? "That is what I wanted to take also." We decided right then that we would go and with some research found out that a class was getting ready to start.

My coworker and I assumed we would get financial aid, because the class was at Community College. However, the Massage Program was not an accredited course, so there was no funding available. Our desire to go was still firm and we asked about options to pay for it. We found out we could pay for the program, one class at a time. We decided to go, purchased books, paid for the first classes, including the required scrubs, linens, and lotions. Finally, I was a student enrolled; after all these years of wanting to go.

The program for the night classes was 14 months long; five nights a week with one Saturday per month. During the time we were in school, my car died. This was not a problem because my coworker, (let's call him Bishop) had his. Months later, he lost his job and soon his car; but this did not stop us. Another of our coworkers would bring us to class and we would catch another classmate home.

When the next set of classes came up, I did not have enough money to pay for them and neither did Bishop. Despite this stumbling block, God whispered to check out my profit-sharing plan. With the funds, I paid my tuition and Bishop's. I purchased one set of books and made him the copies he needed to study with.

The next semester arrived and again there were no funds for me, but Bishop had funds. So, this time he paid for his classes and mine and we again shared books. About halfway through the course, I found out I was on the waiting list for hire by a company that paid great money with excellent benefits. This could have messed up my ability to finish school, however I believed that God would not pull my name off that wait list until after I graduated. Sure, enough we made it through; often, financially by the Grace of God and the skin of our teeth. We completed the course and walked across the stage in late June. August of the same year, the job called. It is funny how neither of us had the means for school but, once we decided to go, God provided.

Looking back on it; I was a single mom making about $9.50 per hour and without financial aid, made it through school. My daughter watched the boys and later my mom helped too. We lost not one but two cars, had to share books, linens, and a practice table, but we made it. "Look at God!" as my daughter says "Won't He do it!

BE CAREFUL WHAT
YOU PRAY FOR

LEFT MY HUSBAND IN 2005. I WANTED MY MARRIAGE TO WORK, BUT once again, I found myself married to someone who was not in the fight. My husband's drug addiction was bigger than he could manage, and our union was no longer worth fighting for alone. Afterall, I needed to protect my children.

I decided when I left that I would not date until after my children were of age. They had been through enough. My first husband had problems with alcohol and would occasionally lose his cool. My second husband was addicted to Crack Cocaine.

In my world, I was striking out with men, and I realized I could not pick them. When I left in 2005, I decided that I would allow God to choose my next person. I asked him to help me be by myself, including curbing my desires to be with a man. I soon settled into a routine, although there were moments of loneliness; I chose not to date. I would interact with coworkers but was closed off to the idea of socially entertaining a boyfriend. When periods of loneliness would creep in, I would hug my pillow at night for comfort. Once you tap into God, He will help you in a variety of ways. Again, He did so through a book by *TD Jakes titled, "Help! I'm Raising My Children Alone."* This book was life changing for me. I loved my children dearly but knew my choosing of men was horrible and I needed to focus more attention on the Gifts God had given me.

During the reading of this book, one day I prayed, "Dear God, I'm not asking you for a husband or a boyfriend, but I am asking for someone that will help me with my kids." "My children need a male role model in their lives since their dads are not active in their world." I was in that moment raising them alone. (I did not know then that God was helping me.)

Later, I suffered an injury and was unable to take care of the upkeep of my yard; cutting grass and things, as my children were too young to do it. While awaiting surgery, Bishop, one of my coworkers asked, "How was my grass?" and I said, "It's a growing." He said, "I'll be by to cut it." I replied, "Thank you."

The first day he came to do the yard, he used my old lawn mower. It was raggedy, but it would work. After cutting the grass he stopped to chat with my children; who were jumping on the trampoline. The following week when he came to cut the grass, Bishop backed in and opened his trunk; inside was a much newer lawnmower. He had purchased it for me. Wow, I was shocked.

Every week Bishop would come like clockwork to do the yard. We began to build a great friendship outside of the workplace. He was good with my kids, would often hang out, and we would watch movies; all of us. Bishop was alone here, his family lived out of state. My sons were the same age as his brothers, so they bonded.

While I was recovering from my injury, I got behind on my car note and to keep from losing it; I made a payment arrangement. I successfully made the first payment as agreed. Imagine my shock, when a coworker called my desk, and told me a tow truck driver was outside and needed my keys. Trying to play it off, I asked, "Who did you say needed my keys?" She repeated, "The tow truck driver." I said, "Oh yeah, I had told them that the van was acting up and they said they'd send someone to pick it up." "Let me go meet him." I was lying through my teeth. When I hung up the phone, my mind was racing. Surely, they did not send someone to get my car; I just made the agreed payment.

Upon walking out the front door, right in front of the store, on a rollback in the loading and unloading zone was my van. The tow truck driver said, "I'm here to repo your car, is there anything you wish to get out of it?" He stated, "He really hated to come to my job." I told him, "I hated that you came to my job too." Embarrassed as all get out, I said, "Just let me get my wallet out." I let everything else go with the van; car seats and all. How could I explain why I had car seats with no car and where would I put them until

I went home. My mind was all over the place. I could not believe they had just picked my car up, after I had made the payment. Had I known, they were going to pick it up anyway; I would not have paid for it. Now, how am I going to get home, I thought to myself.

Bishop my coworker; the same guy that cuts the grass; I will ask him. I did not want to let everyone know what was going on. Since I was on phone duty, I flagged an associate, and asked them to tell Bishop that he had a phone message at the front of the store.

I quickly jotted the following on a piece of paper. "They just repossessed my car, can I get a ride home?" I was hoping when he read it, he would be discreet. In no time, Bishop came to the front to get the message. I said, "You had a phone call. He looked puzzled but took the paper, unfolded it, and read it immediately. "Sure," he said. From that day to this; I never had to ask for another ride.

Each day, Bishop would ask what time he needed to pick me up and I would respond the same way. "Beggars can't be choosy." He took me home from work every day. Some days, he would run me home in between his two jobs. Bishop took me to parent teacher conferences and when my knee had healed, and I needed to work out at the gym; he got a gym membership too.

I asked Bishop one day, "Why did he help me like he did?" He responded, "To me, it's just like breathing." I was twelve years older than him. More and more, he spent time with me and my kids. My sons enjoyed the wrestling moments and my daughter, and her friends enjoyed the laughs and conversation he brought. He would often tease the girls when they had cheerleading tryouts; telling them he had to pay a lot of money to get them on the squad.

One day we were talking, and I was telling him that The Father/Daughter dance was coming up, but my daughter did not want to go. The year before, her dad had left her alone at the dance. Bishop did not really respond other than to say, "That's messed up." The next day he came to me and said, "I thought about it." "I am not sure if Jolie will want to go the dance, but if she does, I will take her." I told him, "I didn't tell you, for you to do it." He said, "I know, but I am offering." I told Jolie and she said, "Yes." We purchased her a new dress, and he bought a new suit. I took pictures and they had an enjoyable time.

Bishop started bridging the gap when it came to things my kids needed.

If their dads did not do it; he would. To prevent my children from being picked on at school; for wearing cheap shoes, he would buy them name brand ones. He even returned items he had purchased for himself; so, my children would not go without.

When my job put me on second shift, it kept my kids from being able to play sports; so, he offered to take them to and from practice. He would come over for meals and just hang out. We played basketball, had snowball fights, and even went to Massage School together.

My kids were comfortable around him. He was faithful in attending church and we later would travel on family vacations together. We were never in a boyfriend/girlfriend type of relationship, although I genuinely loved him.

Bishop had this magic way of knowing if my world was stressed. When things went insane, he would sense it and just show up. We laughed and talked about millions of things, but he could not see us together and we respected our friendship.

Bishop stayed in our lives for over five years, and he would help me with anything. He would even get upset if I were working on a rental house and did not ask him for help. We were best friends, often going on dates that he classified as Business Meetings.

Later in life, I surprised him with tickets to watch his favorite SEC team. Each year after that, we would pick a game to go to and make it a weekend getaway for just me and him. We often shared a room but never a bed. Honestly, we never crossed the line. He was truly a huge blessing and I wished he were mine. I did not hide that I liked him like that, but assured him, I would not jeopardize our friendship. He would laugh and seemed okay with it.

I had to remember my prayer. I did not ask God for a boyfriend or a husband, but someone to help me with my kids and he did just that. By helping them, he helped me, and we are still great friends to this day.

I did get strong enough to start praying, "If he isn't going to be mine God; bless him with someone that will be good to him." Our friendship did eventually go in different directions, but Bishop found his person. They married and had two beautiful children. So, people, I encourage you to think carefully about what you ask God for; although, He may bless you with more, sometimes God just supplies the current need. If this happens, understand, there are things you may need to work on while you are waiting for your person or God may be working on them for you. There is a time and a season for everything. (Ecclesiastes 3:1-8)

(Ecclesiastes 3:1-8NIV)

There is a time for everything, and a season for every activity under the heavens:
2 a time to be born and a time to die, a time to plant and a time to uproot,
3 a time to kill and a time to heal, a time to tear down and a time to build,
4 a time to weep and a time to laugh, a time to mourn and a time to dance,
5 a time to scatter stones and a time to gather them, a time to embrace and a time to refrain from embracing,
6 a time to search and a time to give up, a time to keep and a time to throw away,
7 a time to tear and a time to mend, a time to be silent, and a time to speak,
8 a time to love and a time to hate, a time for war and a time for peace.

THERE'S A BLESSING
IN THE STORM

HAD RECENTLY GONE TO WORK ON NIGHT SHIFT AT THE HOME improvement store. Working at night was my only option since there was no money for day care assistance. Without it, I could not afford childcare. My mom offered to come stay with my children so I could work.

We come from an extensive line of praying folks, and I started showing my children how to pray as well. Each night when my mom would put my children to bed, they prayed that I would be able to get off nights. God answered their prayers quickly. I started the job in November and by February my company told us they were doing away with night shift. What was I to do?

However, before I could produce a solution, my bosses asked to speak with me. "Theodora," they said, "You had emphasized on your application, that you had to have night shift." "We know this change will hurt you, therefore we have decided to collaborate with you, however we need to because we do not want to lose you." (This is an example of God's favor.) I said, "Ok and thank you."

The schedule that would work consisted of me reporting to work at 5am and taking my lunch at 7 am. "Yes," I said, "Lunch at 7am." My mom would put one child on the bus and meet me in the parking lot with the other two. She would go on to work and I would head back across town to drop my daughter off at middle school, the baby at daycare, and then return to work.

At two pm, I would leave work for the day, make a bee line to the daycare, pick my son up, and rush home in time to meet the bus. One wrong move, or a traffic jam and we were in trouble. We were working it out, but summertime was quickly approaching, and I was stressed. How would I pay for summer childcare with no assistance? The closer summer got; the more stressed I became. I had picked up a part time job delivering a weekly circular in the downtown area to help my household, but we were still coming up short. What was I going to do? I spoke with the owner of the day care and inquired if she would discount my cost; provided I would clean and sanitize her facility weekly or however frequently she needed. We agreed to do this. Although I was relieved, I still had to produce a great deal of money.

A coworker was going on vacation and the company asked if I would train at her job so I could cover for her when the schedule required. Her job consisted of changing the prices in the store. I am always eager to learn and was excited to develop new skills. I worked closely with her because next week was her vacation and I would need to show what I had learned.

My coworker's vacation week arrived, and I began my day in her role. I printed off the report, got my labels, and began the process of changing the prices. This was easy; up and down the ladder I went, altering the prices here and there. Then the unthinkable happened. I missed the bottom ring on the ladder. With my foot braced on the floor; all my weight came down on my knee hard. I heard it pop. When my knee popped, it felt like someone had forced air in it. I lowered myself onto the floor and hollered for help.

Soon a fellow employee came, and I asked him to get our safety guy. When he arrived, I told him what happened and he said "OK, let's see what you can do." He asked if I could straighten it. I moved my bent leg to a straightened position; it did not hurt to move it this way. In fact, it felt better, and I told him so, stating, "I may have just jammed it." He then asked if I could stand on it? With him and another guy holding me under my arms, they lifted me to my feet. I could stand; good! Then he said the magic words, "Can you walk?" Being my right side is my dominant side, I started off on the right foot. Right foot on the floor, I stepped; good. Left foot to the floor, I shifted my weight to the left, and my knee gave away like it was Jell-o. I screamed! Not because it hurt, but because it would not support me. They quickly grabbed me and sat me in a chair. We began to go over the options for getting me to the hospital and came to an agreement about me traveling by ambulance. In no time, the EMT's arrived. They loaded and strapped me to a stretcher, right in front of customer service; for all the world to see.

Totally embarrassed, I pulled my ball cap snuggly down to cover my eyes and laughed saying, "You could have picked me up from the curb outside."

At the hospital, x-ray images were taken of the knee; indicating no broken bones, but an MRI revealed a torn anterior cruciate ligament (ACL). I would need surgery to correct it.

People may think that I am unusual when I say this but, injuring my knee was a blessing in disguise. A real blessing in the storm; as I was unsure of how I was going to get through the summer and pay for childcare. My injury was a workman's compensation claim. Because workman's compensation paid weekly, and my job was bi-weekly; the payment was more than my regular check and I was able to stay home with my kids during the remainder of the summer. By the time school was starting back up, I was able to return to work.

God had been in my mess. It was also during this injury that I stood in my kitchen on crutches; trying to figure out how to wash dishes, how to hold a plate and crutches at the same time. I thought, what if this injury had been permanently life altering? Would there be things I wanted to do but had not done yet? This became my prescription for living. I decided to go to Massage School and stop thinking about it. After that injury, anything I wanted to do, I did.

My theory is…It is only too late when you are six feet under. I often say, *"Every day that breath is given; is the opportunity to change, be better, try something new. Don't waste it!"*

FAITH WITHOUT WORKS

I t was early one Sunday morning, and I was looking at the Newspaper as I often did. I would browse through the sale papers, clip coupons, glance or read the articles; making sure to check the classified ads. Classified ads were the way to search for employment back in the day.

There, in a half page ad was one of the largest manufacturing companies in our city. Not only one of the largest, but a great paying one. This company was a deep desire of most people in the area; to become their employer. Right on the front of the classified section was their mini solicitation; with instructions to cut out and mail in. The job request stated that applicants must be able to work all shifts. I made sure I applied.

Upon filling out the request, I knew I could not work every shift because I was a single parent. So, I prayed and asked God if my application were selected for hire, would He please let me work first shift. I placed the solicitation in the mail; not thinking any more of it. Months went by and I got a call from my sister. She stated, the company had called; asking for me. I was confused as to why they called her and not me. However, I was grateful just the same. She gave me the name and number of who to speak with.

Quickly, I phoned the lady. She stated they would like me to take a test and gave me the date and time. She said, "Be prepared to stay for three hours." I responded, "Yes ma'am and thank you."

The test day came, and my children cheered me on. I arrived at the hotel where they were giving the exam. There were people everywhere; all waiting to take this test. The process was well orchestrated. We stood in line based on our last names; to verify with a photo ID. We shuffled into rooms with classroom seating and huge screens like at the movies. There were different tests given of assorted styles.

The tests were not what I call an exam of high intelligence but more of skill, technicality, and the ability to follow directions. If you passed the test, you would advance to the second round. The results of this test would arrive in the mail. When I got home my children asked how I did. I said "I'm not sure, all I know is God pulled my application, so I am in."

Close to six weeks went by and then a letter from the company arrived. I had advanced to round two of testing. I had to go to the same hotel, where again, there were hundreds of people. They passed too. At the end of this session, I did not feel as confident, but responded the same to my children. "I'm not sure how I did but, God pulled my application, so I am in." The results of the second test would also arrive by mail. If you passed round two, there would be an offer for a third test. I thought to myself, Lord have mercy, wonder how many assessments there are?

The letter finally arrived, stating that I had passed this test also. The third exam would be a job assimilation test and it required that I come into the facility. Once checked in by security, I was issued a team-colored jersey and placed in a group of other candidates. Detailed instructions were given, and we were shuffled like children in a school line, into a room where managers sat around the wall with clipboards, jotting notes and judging our performance. The assimilation test involved five to six candidates on a team, manually attempting to build a product, keeping up with orders, and communicating with one another in a controlled environment. The timer, production pace, and the looking eyes of judgment made this taxing and intense. By the time it was over, I really felt like I had not done so well but responded again the same way to my children. "I'm not sure, but God pulled my application, so I'm in."

During the time of testing for this excellent job, I was employed and going to Massage School. After months of waiting, an offer of employment was made, but I was waitlisted for a start date. At that point, I knew within my being that God was not going to pull my name off the list until I had completed my Massage program. Exactly like I said, I graduated from Massage School in May and by August of the same year, the company called, offering me a position, starting on first shift.

Look at God! When we place our faith in Him, there is no telling what

He can do for us and on our behalf. Although I enjoyed my current job, this new position was starting at $7.00 more per hour. As a single mom, I would have been out of my mind to turn it down. I received this blessing, and it was great. My faith grew with each test; realizing myself alone I could have failed, but with God, all things are possible to those who believe. (Mark 10:27) God did not let me down.

Jesus looked at them and said, "With man this is impossible, but not with God; all things are possible with God." (Mark 10:27NIV)

TERMINATED

MY SON WAS EXTREMELY SICK; BACK AND FORTH TO THE DOCTORS and now a specialist. The diagnosis, "Too much stomach acid." The doctor described it as if you slid on concrete, tearing off your skin and then someone pouring rubbing alcohol on the wound. This was my son's stomach and throat (esophagus) area; completely raw. No wonder he rolled on the floor with fist clenched as tears streamed down his face. We had a diagnosis but not a quick fix. A round of medications, trial, and error to see what will soothe. He was only 15 years old. Yes, he stood almost six feet tall and weighed close to 165 lbs., but was still a child.

Not just any child; he was mine and I was going to stick with him. So, when my job said I did not qualify for FMLA, and if I missed another night out of work, they would suspend me for three days. "Well, suspend me then." I said, "Do what you got to do, this is my child, and he is sick." And so was I. The stress of him being ailing had taken a toll on my body as well. I felt like I had a butcher knife stabbed in my back literally and my blood pressure was way too high. It's no wonder my doctor took me out of work. Now I can take care of my son and myself.

When I turned the doctor's note into the nurse on duty; I explained that the first two days of the note was the same time I had been suspended from work. I asked if that was a problem. The nurse on duty, in the Medical Department; counted it up and stated that the note was for seven days, and that was enough time to qualify for leave. Two days later, my paperwork for my leave of absence arrived by mail; with the words approved and instructions on when to return. It also stated if unable to do so; to get an extension note from the doctor and bring it into the medical department.

Okay, everything is a go, I thought. Day three, at 2 am in the morning, my phone rings. One of my close friends Jessie was on the phone; crying in full blown tears. "What in the world is wrong with you?" I asked. She said, "Your job is on the board, you've been terminated." "They have fired you." Very Calmly, I said, "Ok." She asked, "If I heard what she said?" I said, "Yes, I heard you." "My question to you is why are you crying?" She explained, "This is your job, you're a single mom, what are you going to do?" I responded, "You forget who I serve." "God has taken care of me when I have had great paying jobs and no job." "He will see me through this."

It was devastating, because in the middle of my son's illness, I lost my job, my income, not to mention later found out my insurance and benefits too. But God...

I trusted Him to see me through. Amid my son's illness, I knew from doctor appointments, administering medicines, on top of him not feeling well; holding down a full-time position would be impossible. I said, "God, I cannot work a regular job right now, with my son sick, but I am willing to do whatever." "You gave me skills; help me." That is exactly what He did.

I was able to pay bills better with no job than when I had one. I kept my word and was willing to do whatever and did by cleaning carpet, cleaning houses, cleaning office buildings, painting, performing clothing alterations, repairing washers and dryers, making curtains, sewing quilts, flipping houses for property owners, baking cakes and desserts, fixing faucets, toilets, doorbells, braiding hair, even driving cars in an auction. With God's help, I took every legal opportunity to make a dollar. YouTube became my classroom. If there was a video on something I did not know how to do, I would study. If the video were five minutes long, I knew I could do it in under thirty. I became a Jill of many trades and ended up having a profitable painting and cleaning business. Where there is a will there is a way; especially when you know God.

> Trust in the Lord with all your heart and lean not on your own understanding; 6 in all your ways submit to him and he will make your paths straight. (Proverbs 3:5-6 NIV)

SOWING SEEDS

HAVE YOU EVER HEARD OLD FOLKS SAY, "YOU'RE GOING TO REAP what you sow," especially when a child was misbehaving. They would often scold them and follow up with those words indicating, whatever you did would show up in your life later; especially when you have your own children.

As I acquired more birthdays, I realized how true of a statement it is. Not only in relation to dreadful things but also good things. I am a firm believer in Reaping and Sowing. How you treat people will come back to you. So, if you fill your days with laughter and kindness towards another person, guess what? You will reap laughter and kindness. If you are a helper by nature; giving of yourself whether time, money, or both; you will reap the same.

I always say, *"You do not plant a field of corn and reap potatoes." "What you put in is what you get out."* In saying that, I decided to make the effort to sow into my future, as well as the future of my kids and my children's children. Your harvest time may not be from the seeds you planted but from those planted before you. (Galatian 6:7)

As my business grew, I went out of my way for my customers. I called it sowing seeds. I rearranged furniture, hung pictures, took them to doctors' appointments, and picked up medication. Whatever way I could assist them; I did. Ninety percent of my customers were over the age of seventy-three.

[7] Do not be deceived: God can not be mocked.
A man reaps what he sows.
[8] Whoever sows to please their flesh, from
the flesh will reap destruction.
whoever sows to please the spirit, from the Spirit will reap eternal life.

> [9] *Let us not become weary in doing good, for at*
> *the proper time we will reap a harvest*
> *If we do not give up.*
> [10] *Therefore, as we have opportunity, let us do*
> *good to all people, especially to those*
> *Who belong to the family of believers. (Galatians 6:7-10NIV)*

Now sowing seeds came easy for me because I am a helper and giver by nature. Even as a young child; I easily shared things, I believed in people, and would help them any way I could. It was nothing for me as a single mom to share with another mom; the food in my kitchen.

If there were two boxes of spaghetti, she got one and I kept one. If I had two packages of meat, she would get one and I kept one. I would split whatever I had. It may have been my last and no money to replenish it, but God honored it, and I never ran out. The bible says God loves a cheerful giver. (2Corinthians 9:7)

> *Each of you should give what you have decided in your*
> *heart to give, not reluctantly or under compulsion, for*
> *God loves a cheerful giver. (2 Corinthians 9:7 NIV)*

Cheerful for me may not have been the right word, I just was not going to have anyone hungry on my watch. How wrong am I, to not share; when I have it to give? (Proverbs 3:27-28)

> [27] *Do not withhold good from those to whom it is due, when it is in your power to act.*
>
> [28] *Do not say to your neighbor, "Come back tomorrow and I'll give it to you"_ when you already have it with you. (Proverbs 3:27-28 NIV)*

Therefore, I often sowed into the lives of others and kept it to myself. I was not a person to go around bragging about what I had done for someone else; it was always between me and them. (Matthew 6:3) I sowed kindness, love, and respect. I sowed financially if I could. I spoke words of encouragement, gave pep talks, advice if asked, sent up prayers on behalf of others, cheered them on in pursuit of dreams; and boy was I glad I did. I reaped in unusual ways.

But when you give to the needy, do not let your left hand
know what your right hand is doing, ⁴ so that your giving
may be in secret. Then your Father, who sees what is done
in secret, will reward you. (Matthew 6:3-4NIV)

Due to kindness and compassion shown to a fellow single mom, whether it was gas, food, washing powders, or wisdom; it came back to me. When I lost my job, she expressed to people the things I had done to bless her. In doing so, she often brought me envelopes with funds overflowing, from people who wished to bless me during my crisis.

One day she called with another blessing. I have more money for you. She said, "You will never guess, who told me to make sure I did not leave before he went by the bank. (There was a bank inside the building). He wanted to give me something for you. I asked, "Who?" She said, "This guy, (we are going to call) Jeffrey and mentioned she was amazed that he did." I told her, "I was not surprised, because we are good friends." She said, "For real, he does not talk to many people, and he is friends with you?" I said "Yes, you can never guess who I may be friends with." I honestly and genuinely try to treat people as people and because of that I have friends from all levels of society. We are all created in Gods image (Genesis 1:26) and you never know when you could be entertaining an angel. (Hebrews 13:2)

So created mankind in his own image, in the
image of God he created them; male and female
he created them. (Genesis 1:27 NIV)

Do not forget to show hospitality to strangers, for
by doing so some people have shown hospitality to
angels without knowing it. (Hebrews 13:2 NIV)

Jeffrey gave her a very thick envelope. One so thick; she could not bear for me to leave her presence without opening it. Curiosity had gotten the best of her. She wanted to know how much it was. Inside the envelope was several one-hundred-dollar bills. As I shuffled the bills and counted; she counted too. $ 700.00 enough to pay the rent. Jeffrey was not the only one that had blessed me with a large amount.

A lady gave me a hundred dollars for a simple sleeve alteration on a dress that would have cost $ 10.00. On another day, this same lady, for a different type of alteration left once again $ 100.00. Then she donated $100.00, and with the fourth donation of $100.00 she left a note. It said, "Months ago, God told me to give you $400.00" She asked, (speaking to God) "Ok, now?" He told her to wait. She waited awhile and I went out for knee surgery. She asked God, "Now?" Again, He told her to wait. She said she was disappointed that I had returned to work, and she still had not given it to me. So, she asked God again, "Do I give it now?" He said again to wait. When this happened, with my son getting sick and losing my job, God said, "Give it to her now." This is the last hundred. She also stated, "I am telling you this, because God told me to give you the money months ago." "He instructed me to wait until the appropriate time." Therefore, God had already prepared, knew this was going to happen, and He has a plan.

I was amazed and grateful for all the blessings, but really moved by the note she sent. The season of losing my job caught me off guard but not God; the note confirmed that. He had been working behind the scenes; lining up people to help me along the way. (1 Corinthians 2:9)

> *However, as it is written: "What no eye has seen, what no ear has heard, and what no human mind has conceived," – the things God has prepared for those who love him- (1 Corinthians 2:9 NIV)*

A RAM IN THE BUSH

N OT ONLY HAD I JUST LOST MY JOB, BUT MY CHILD WAS ALSO battling an illness on top of the stomach issues. He began showing normal cold / flu like symptoms. His brother Ethan was sick as well and already had an appointment with the doctor. I called to see if they could see Solomon too. Thank God they quickly agreed and said the boys could be seen at 10 am. I thanked the lady and started getting ready.

Within moments, the phone rang, and the caller ID showed the same doctor's office. I answered, and the lady on the phone asked if I had my insurance card handy. I said, "Sure." She then asked if I could read off the numbers? I told her yes and proceeded to do so. "Ms. Gray," she said, "I was hoping that there was a different card; they have cancelled your insurance." Tears began to flow as I explained, "Since Solomon got sick, I lost my job trying to care for him and was hoping they hadn't cancelled the insurance yet." She was nice and compassionate, so I asked her, "How much the visit would cost; without insurance?" "$120.00", she replied. I knew I had about $30.00 to my name. What was I going to do? I told her to let me see if I can borrow it and to please hold the appointment. This was another blow to my already weighted heart. November 19, 2015, was the day the insurance ceased. How did I lose my job on the 19th and they cancel my insurance the very same day. In my mind; I calculated that my employer had made it a point to make sure that everything ceased on that day. Wow, here my child is sick, I have lost my job and they have already cut off my insurance. What in the world? The tears began to flow uncontrollably, as I went into the back bedroom. I did not want my sons to know. I especially did not want Solomon to think this was his fault; because it was not.

I prayed to God, "What am I going to do?" "I've got to get him seen and I don't know how I'm going to pay for it." "Tell me who to ask for the money." "God please!" Within moments, Ken came to mind. Ken was a coworker and a good friend. Our families have bonded over the years, and we often refer business to one another. He has a carpet cleaning business and I have the painting and cleaning. No sooner than Ken come to mind; the phone that was in my hand began to ring. When I looked down to see who was calling, it was Ken. I answered the phone and the first thing he said was "What's wrong?" Did he hear it in my voice or did God tell him to call? I explained, still sniffling that they had cancelled my insurance. I said Solomon was sick, and I only had a portion of the money to get him seen by the doctor. Ken asked, "How much the visit would be, what time, and where?" I told him the location and 10 am. He responded, "I'll meet you there." I got the boys up and ready to go. Just like he said, Ken met me at the office. He spoke and walked up to the clerk, swiped his card and back out the door he went. God had sent me an angel just in time. A ram in the bush as old folks say. (Genesis 22:13)

Abraham looked up and there in a thicket he saw a ram caught by its horns. He went over and took the ram and sacrificed it as a burnt offering instead of his son. (Genesis 22:13NIV)

THE NETTIE POT

GOD HAD SHOWED UP DURING MY CRISIS, INCLUDING WHEN I found out that there was no longer any insurance. Without a job my income was next to none. The few dollars I had needed to be stretched beyond measure.

One of the things I needed desperately to help my sons was a Nettie Pot. The Nettie pot was beneficial to wash the nasal cavities when there was sinus issues or congestion from a cold. Since both boys had nasty nasal symptoms; this would be of major help.

I had a new bottle of cold medicine with the receipt. In my mind, I thought it would be good to return this bottle to the store and use the funds to purchase a Nettie Pot. The drug store was just minutes from our home, and I frequented there often. In I walked, with the cold medicine and receipt in my hand; no bag.

It took me a few minutes to find the shelf with the Nettie Pots. Upon close inspection, I realized even returning the cold medicine; I still would not have enough money to purchase the pot. I quickly found the manager and showed him the medicine and my receipt. This was proof that I had purchased it. I did not want anyone to think I had stolen the medicine. I explained that I did not have enough money to buy the Nettie Pot but was going home to see if I could scrape up enough money to get it. If so, I will return to the store after getting the money, and I will return the medicine and buy the pot," I told the Manager.

He smiled and said, "Go get whatever you need and meet me at the counter." He said, "Ma'am, you are a regular customer in our store, and it would not be nice to have a customer such as yourself, not have what she needs for her sick child."

He rang up the Nettie Pot under some code. I signed the receipt and out the door I went; thanking him ever so much and thanking God. Once again, God had provided a Ram in the Bush.

ANONYMOUSLY SENT

O FTEN, MY FRIEND JESSIE WOULD CALL SAYING SHE HAD MORE money from coworkers and friends. Over and over, I received hundreds of dollars in donations to help us pay bills, buy groceries, and medicine. The people on my job had really, really blessed us and I was profoundly grateful. I still get teary eyed thinking of the favor that came our way during this crisis. Even unusual moments like the day I went to the mailbox.

The driveway is a good distance from our house and when I am coming home, I often drive up to the mailbox and then pull into the driveway. However, on days when I am already home or failed to stop on my way in, I would walk to the box. On this day, I walked. Whenever there is mail in the box, I always fan through the letters quickly glancing and sorting it in my head.

There amid the bills was a legal-size envelope, handwritten, and addressed to me. Naturally, the first letter I opened was the one handwritten. Inside was a plain white piece of paper with the words, "I thought you may need this." There were two gift cards inside, one to the drug store and one to the grocery store. There was not a name in the letter; and I did not recognize the handwriting. In that moment, I remembered that there was a return address written on the envelope. I quickly flipped the letter over to see who it was from. To my surprise, the letter was addressed to me; from me. As if I had mailed it to myself.

I instantly sent up a thank you to God and told Him to thank the person that sent it; only He knows who it is. The gift cards were right on time. God does, always provide. (2Corinthians 9:8)

> *And God is able to bless you abundantly, so that in all*
> *things at all times, having all that you need, you will*
> *abound in every good work. (2 Corinthians 9:8 NIV)*

THE SET UP

FOR YEARS, I STRUGGLED AS A SINGLE PARENT, LEARNING VALUABLE lessons along the way. This has molded me into the person I am today. Due to the life moments that I endured; I became the relief person for someone else. I remember needing someone to get my children off the school bus. Therefore, if someone needed their child picked up and I was available; I would help. I recall the times my job was in jeopardy because my children were sick, and I had to miss work. So, whenever my friends or family's children were sick, and I was available to assist; I would offer to keep them.

Even during the summer, when I worked third shift, I would help my friends with their summer needs of childcare. People often asked why I helped everyone out? I explained, "I never forgot the many times, I needed help; so why not help someone else."

At one point, I recall running a small bus route with my vehicle. I had Ethan and Solomon both under three years of age and I owned an extra-long passenger van. Every day, I would load the boys in the van, then pick up Jolie (my daughter) and Savannah (my neighbors' daughter) from their Charter School. Then we would pick up Jasmine (another of my friends' daughters) and go across town to pick up her brother Jaz, from his school. Dre and Paris were the last of the kids to be picked up from High School. This was a daily routine.

When there was a holiday break from school, my friends would call up and see if their child could come over for the day. My response was always yes. It may come with a clause, to the effect of, "Today is a painting day, so send them in clothes they can get paint on," or "If we were working in the yard, dress accordingly."

I just loved children, especially my niece and nephew. They are true joys and on this day, I needed to help my sister by taking my nephew to the orthodontist. In the office, the Holy Spirit pushed me to inquire; what would be the cost for my sons' braces, if I needed to pay for them out of pocket? Both of my sons needed braces badly, but I had lost my job. I knew at the end of the year; I would be able to withdraw money from my profit-sharing plan, and that would cover the cost.

When I inquired, the lady said, "Do you not have insurance?" I replied, "No, my son got sick, and I lost my job." She then asked, "If we were on Medicaid?" and I said, "Yes, ma'am." She responded, "If there is a need for the braces medically; then Medicaid will pay at 100%." I lit up like a Christmas tree, I knew my sons would qualify medically. We scheduled the assessment which included a series of images taken of each son; from different angles. "They should approve them," she said. She also explained, the braces are paid for as soon as they are placed on the teeth. Even if you lose your benefits later, all the adjustments and treatments are fully covered.

Sure enough, Medicaid approved my sons for their braces. God had just granted us a $15,000.00 blessing, while I was helping someone else. It was not by chance; I heard "the whisper" to ask how much the cost would be to fix their teeth. Another example, of how God works. You have no idea how thrilled I was on the day their braces were placed on their teeth. As each son came from the back of the orthodontist office, I said, "Let me see your braces." Other parents have done this as well; however, for me, that metal smile was priceless. It sealed God's blessing. It was the stamp from God himself saying, "It is done!" "They are paid for." Even now, I tease them by saying, "Show me them choppers; let me see that smile." When they smile, my heart smiles. God did it again!

A BLESSING IN DISGUISE

L IFE HAD TAKEN A TURN, BUT WE WERE SURVIVING. MY SON WAS desiring to return to school, and it was also time for me to resume a regular 40-hour work routine.

I had truly been blessed. God had taken my work ethic and combined his grace and mercy. We were making it. I was operating my painting and cleaning business as well as cleaning offices on the side. Add in that I was also drove cars through the auction two nights a week. Not to mention, I had just finished a semester of college and made the Dean's list.

I had balanced the hectic schedule, so why not resume the normal one. Assessing my needs, I decided working night shift would be best. I found the perfect job. The ad stated the work hours were 9pm to 5am, with pay starting at $13.00 per hour; so, I applied. In a short amount of time, I was interviewing for the position.

I always had the confidence that I could land the job, I just needed my application pulled. Since I was at the interviewing stage, the job was mine. I knew I could sell myself as a good fit for the company and boy did I.

There was one issue though; during the interview process I was informed that 5 am was not a confirmed time to end the day, but rather, one would work until all orders were completed. I asked, "Worst case scenario, what is the latest time we would get off?" The company responded, "Around 7 or 7:30 am." I said, "Ok." Confirmation came in, that I had indeed sold them; and they offered me the job. Instead of the pay starting at $13.00 per hour, they were going to start me at $17.00. Wow, what a blessing.

On the first day of orientation; they informed all the new hires that our start time was 7 pm instead of nine. Several people asked if we would get off earlier and their response was no. Everyone would still be required to work until all orders were complete. Now this was a real curve for me and very discouraging. I am a firm believer that people need to be specific, employers included. Do not run an ad for one thing and then later say something different.

My years of working in warehouse and distribution environments, had given me a huge skillset of driving forklift equipment. Upon being assigned to the department; I let them know I could drive equipment if needed. They were thrilled and then they said, "My start time would begin even earlier." I told them, "No, you've already changed it, and we aren't changing it again." The manager said, "They still needed me to drive equipment, so they would allow me to remain at the 7 pm time."

On day two, instead of the employees getting off no later than 7:30 am, they got off at 10 am. What in the world? To report to work at 7pm, but not get off until 10 am, and do this five days a week; no, this is not going to work. I asked the dept manager if this was normal. I explained, there would be no need for me to continue training if it was. He quickly assured me that 10 am was not normal, it was because they currently were short staffed. He stated once their staffing needs were met, the schedule would resume back to normal. I again said, "Ok."

I was really annoyed but was also stuck. I had to provide for my kids and did not want to be without a job. I frequently tell people, *"If you have a job, you can get a job, but if you do not have a job, you cannot buy one,"* so quitting was not an option.

A day or two later, I had dozed off watching television and when the alarm went off to pick up my son from work; I jumped up quickly thinking I was late. I noticed at that time my balance was off.

On my way to get Ethan, I was aware that the dizzy feeling had not worn off. Normally, if I were off balance from jumping up; it would resolve itself in a few moments. However, tonight was different. Oh, my goodness I thought; I am only four days in on this job and I drive equipment that goes high in the air. I am strapped to my forklift, so I can step out onto pallets and select items; not the ideal job to do while dizzy. All my mind could imagine was one of the guys coming down an aisle to find me swinging upside down in the air because I had lost my balance.

I decided to call the job, explain that I woke up dizzy, and see if they would let me do another job tonight instead. I was instructed to tell my manager when I arrived. On my way to work things got worse; so bad that I could not walk in a straight line. I felt like if they saw me this dizzy; they would realize I was not just calling out for the sake of calling out. It was all I could do to make it to the employee entrance of the building. I picked up the phone and requested a manager. By the time the manager got to where I was; I had my head braced on the wall; trying to steady myself. It did not take him long to realize I was severely off balance. I told him, "I had come to work with the intention to work, but I am too dizzy to do so, and would be in fact calling someone to pick me up; as I could no longer drive." He helped me get to the breakroom and told me to call HR in the morning. He also said, "We don't have a sick policy, they'll tell you what to do."

"Man, this is in usual," I thought to myself. "I just started work with this nice company." "I am four days in, and this sick; dizzy-wise and on top of it; they don't have a sick policy." "I'm still in the probationary period, and they're probably going to let me go."

The next morning, I was seen at the doctor's office with hopes of them giving me something that would solve the woozy feeling. Instead, I was given meds and taken out of work with a diagnosis of Vertigo. Vertigo is the proper term for the dizziness I described. Well, there goes my job; I thought; I just got it. My supervisor already said, "They don't have a sick policy," but told me to call HR.

I followed instructions and placed the call. Surprisingly, the lady was extremely nice and told me, "Yes ma'am, we don't have a sick policy." "We can give you a leave of absence under FMLA." I said, "Okay," and then she said, "Your benefits kicked in on day one of your employment, so you will receive full pay for the first four months." "If you need to be out longer than the four months, your pay will drop to 80% of pay, for the remaining two months." "Oh, my goodness", I thought, "Did God just do that?"

My vertigo lasted almost six full months, with me having to take physical therapy to re-train my brain; to adapt to what I saw. This unsteadiness was not the normal kind of world spinning, nausea, and vomiting. The kind I suffered would have me grabbing hold of things; trying to steady my footing. Turning my head would cause me to feel like I was going to fall. I described it as my head was a balloon caught in the breeze; not able to control its movement. I could be having an okay day; walk in a store, and within minutes I would be sick to my stomach; become way off balance and immediately get a headache.

I had to keep a journal to help identify the triggers; lights bothered me, high pitched sounds, and riding in a car. There was even a difference noticed between riding on a city road, with frequent turns, and changes of direction, vs. a highway road whose course was more direct. Even the weather affected me. If the sun was out; it was a great day. However, if the sky was overcast / cloudy, it was a bad day. Any background that had a whitish tone irritated me, like my neighbor's cement garage that is painted white and is right outside my window.

I even told the nurse, at my eye exam who was swaying side to side while she talked, "Lady, I can't watch you, you're making me sick", as I threw my hands over my eyes; in an attempt to stop the dizziness. She gave me a look, like how dare you, until I apologized; explaining, I was having vertigo and her swaying movements were making me queasy.

My sister, who often took me to my appointments, had to hold me by my clothes; so, I wouldn't drift into a car or fall. It was a different kind of experience. Even my physical therapist explained that the treatments to re-train me to what I saw, would also make me sick (dizzy). She said, "If I was wiped out and had to lie down afterwards, I had over did it." My first exercise required me to look at a tongue depressor with a smiley face on the end, focusing on the face, and move my arm left to right for 15 repetitions. Three movements and I was wiped out; feeling horrible and needing to lie down. Each day, repeat the exercises again until I built up to 15.

During this time, I was referred to doctors and they ran all kinds of tests. Finally, a neurologist determined that I was having silent migraines; triggered by fluorescent and ultraviolent lighting. I had to wear a ball cap and sunglasses everywhere I went. Think I was not looking ridiculous. This was before Covid; nothing looks ridiculous now.

Before I had started this job, I was finishing a semester of college, along with working part- time jobs. Over the years, I learned every way possible to legally create income. Since I had to drive my son to school every day, as bus service was not available; to save on gas I would wait for him. If I was going to wait, why not attend classes. The extra money left from my financial aid would help pay bills and bridge the shortage of income. Every day I would drop my son off at school, go to class, run clean a customer, pick my son up and head to the auction or clean offices. Sometimes it would be both. This vertigo spell shut me down.

However, my son could now drive himself to school. I had just finished the semester and was getting ready to start the next term when the dizziness started. Due to this job, I now had full wages and I could rest and recover, without having to worry about how we were going to make it. The cleaning and painting side of my business had to be put on hold, but God provided.

My son graduated in June and my benefits ceased in June. Look at God; He will show up and sometimes even show out. What a blessing!

LEARNING TO LISTEN

ONE DAY MY MIDDLE SON ETHAN, SAID "MOMMA, I WANT YOU TO listen to something." I said, "Okay." He said, "You're not going to be able to follow it at first, your mind will wander." "When you find your mind drifting to other things; stop the audio and back it up to what you recall." "Do this over and over until, you have honestly listened to the entire message." I said, "Okay." He said, "Please promise me you will listen to it." "Sure, I said, send it to me."

Over the years, as much as I would love to think or want to say; my relationship with my sons, is not as close as my daughter and me. It is not that I do not want it to be, and the boys desire it to be also; we just communicate differently. The book *"Men Are From Mars, Women Are From Venus, The Classic Guide To Understanding The Opposite Sex" by John Gray, Ph. D.* could not be more accurate when it comes to communicating.

Eager to build the adult-child parent bond; I was determined to listen to what my son sent. As the audio played on my phone; I listened intently. The person's voice was easy to follow, they spoke with enthusiasm; occasionally joking and provoking laughter.

Boy, this is going to be easy; I thought. Wait, wait, what did he say? That quickly, my mind had jumped to buying groceries, and what I was going to fix for supper. I caught myself and remembered what my son had said. I backed up the audio recording and started it again. Listening carefully, I thought this was useful information, but in moments; I was thinking of budgeting bills, who I was going to pay first, running errands, etc.

I realized that although the audio was playing, and I could hear the words, because my mind drifted; I was not actually listening. Even though

I could hear, without thinking about what the person was saying; I was not recalling or retaining what was said.

Determined to complete the audio, I stopped and backed the message up so many times; I could no longer count. By the time I was finished; a new world had opened. The audio message was by a motivational speaker named Zig Ziglar on setting goals.

Once I learned how to listen; my spirit and soul could be fed. Fascinated with the words the messenger spoke; I began to grow and see life differently. I started listening in the car to motivational messages instead of the radio. Zig Ziglar, Les Brown, and Andrew Carnegie were my beginning favorites. When I developed the ability to listen with reasoning ears, I began to dream more for my life; learning how to control my thinking.

Because I have a true faith in God, when a motivational speaker referenced things from the bible; I was hooked. Soon I became aware that if I change my thinking; I could change my life. In no time, my inspirational speakers included Dr. Myles Munroe, Joel Osteen, Steve Harvey, Denzel Washington, Steven Furtick, and many more. I became almost addicted to the messages, motivating myself and others.

Years ago, I also read a book titled *"The Secret," written by Rhonda Byrne* which is simply the law of attraction; how to manifest the things you desire. The book was later made into a movie. Although, visually, I could see and hear the message; it was not until after I learned how to listen, that I went back and watched the movie again. This time I paused it with pen and paper in hand; trying to make sure I recorded every detail.

For me to retain information, I jot notes, highlight features, even taking the time to write something that really speaks to me on my arm until I get home and write it on my bathroom mirror. I use dry erase markers which wipe completely away with glass cleaner.

Changing my thinking, changed my world. As I travelled from customer to customer, I spoke to myself; by way of motivation. The words that I learned to build my spirit and self-esteem; I began to share with others. As more ideas came to mind, whether they were to motivate, manifest or to speak to my being; I listened and grew.

If God had not told my son to share the audio message with me, the person I have become and is still evolving into may not have existed. At least not at this current time. I encourage you as you read these pages to learn new ways to inspire yourself and grow. God has a plan for you, (Jeremiah 29:11) and you have no idea who He will use to help you get there.

> *"For I know the plans I have for you," declares the Lord,*
> *"plans to prosper you and not to harm you, plans to give*
> *you hope and a future." (Jeremiah 29:11 NIV)*

IT'S BIGGER THAN YOU THINK

L IFE WAS BUSY, BUT WE WERE MANAGING. MY BUSINESS WAS DOING good. I was painting and cleaning. My son was courageous and had desired to return to school following his illness. He was playing football again and seemed happy.

Every morning we would go and clean an office before he started his school day. We shared a car, and I would drop him off at school on days there was not a conflict in scheduling. When there was, I would give him my car to drive, and I would coordinate between my other two children; to borrow their cars. We were making it work. This day was no different. Solomon was to take my Kia to school and drop his girlfriend off at work on his way. Her grandmother was in the hospital, and she needed our help. Of course, we would; as people have helped us. I told my son; take my car, and I will drop your brother off at work and use his car to go to clean my customer.

Everything started off smoothly. I had arrived at my client's home and started cleaning when the phone rang, it was my son. Momma he said, "We were running behind, so I wouldn't be late to school, (Solomon's girl we will call her) Sunflower has the car." "Can you pick me up from school this afternoon, so we can get the car?" "Sure, I said, thanks for letting me know."

Not fifteen minutes later, he called back frantic. Sunflower said, "The car will not start." "What, where's she at?" I asked. "Please call her momma, he said, she's scared." "Okay, okay," I replied, quickly moving through my customer's house. I let them know I was stopping and would be back. "There was a problem with the car my son was driving," I told them.

While trying to calm Sunflower down, I was assessing where she was; compared to me. Shoot, over an hour away. I think fast, realizing my aunt and uncle lived right down from where the car had stalled. I tell Sunflower, "I am going to try to send family up to where you are; until I can get there."

I got my uncle on the phone and told him what was going on and asked if he would come up and stay with her until I arrived. He said, "Sure."

I felt if I were a young girl, pulled over on the side of the road with a stalled car; I would rather not be alone. Sunflower was relieved. I had roadside assistance, but was not sure if they would assist us if someone else was driving; so, I waited until I was on the scene to phone it in.

To my surprise, the company said they did not see that I had roadside assistance even though I was paying extra for it on my bill. I send up a quick prayer, "God, please send me a tow truck driver that can move my vehicle at a price I can afford." I pulled out my phone and searched for cheap tow truck drivers near me. One name stood out over the others. It was not in bold print or italics, yet his name stood out just the same.

I placed the call, told him where the car was and that I needed it picked up from here and taken to Essex (30 + miles away.) When I asked, "How much he would tow it for, he said, one-hundred dollars." I asked, "For real?" He said, "Yes." I said, "Thank you, thank you."

I read off the name of the street the car had broken down on and the closest house number that I could see; so, he could find us. Upon putting the address in his GPS, he said, "Oh, you're out farther than I thought." I asked him, "If it was going to cost me more." He said, "Normally, it would, but the price I quoted is the price we're going with." I told him, "He would go far in business with that mindset," and thanked him again. I also said, "I would try to give him a little extra."

I did not have that much money but called my daughter and she sent it immediately. The driver kept his word and picked up my car from the location; taking it home. He was not a fancy, big name tow company. He had an old truck painted plain black. Because he was so nice, I told him if he ever wanted his business name on it, to talk to my son Ethan; who does collision and body work and can paint cars. He was thrilled.

I called my regular mechanic to come work on it and hopefully find out what was wrong. I anticipated it was the alternator, but Mr. Sims, the mechanic never returned my call. My children by this time, were all frazzled.

"That was the only car we had to get back and forth", they said. Solomon had school out of the area of bus service, I had my business, and we were already sharing a car. What are we going to do?" they asked.

Very firmly, in a positive tone, I told them, "I am not worried, watch how God is going to work this thing out." "You are going to be surprised." I did not have a clue as to how God would handle it, I just knew that He would.

I ended up having to have the car towed to another mechanic shop and blessed the same guy that helped me before; with my business again. Engine seized was the findings. What? I called Kia because there was a recall for the same year, make, and model as mine. Kia said that they could not take another businesses word for it, they would need to check it out themselves. So, I called the same tow truck guy back; a third time, to have the Kia taken from the car shop to the Kia dealership.

Kia confirmed the engine was seized and would get a price list together to repair it; only to later tell me my car was manufactured at a different facility and the recall did not cover my vehicle.

I was making payments on this Kia, and they still denied fixing it. Had my daughter's name not been on it; I would not have made another payment, but protecting her credit I would.

I told Kia, "If you can lay down at night and be at peace knowing my car has the same problem, that's fine, but one way or another my car will be fixed." Two days later, Kia called back, only to tell me again they would not help me. I told them, "I heard you two days ago." I did not need them to repeat it!

Days later, the dealership called and said, "They heard, I had a seized engine and what if I just traded it in on a new one?" "Fine with me," I thought. I really did not care if the problem got solved. They told me, "They didn't want mine, but would add the remaining balance to the new car." "All we had to do, was get my daughter to cosign."

By this time, I had found another car to drive and paid for it in cash. I told them, "I am not desperate, you don't understand." "I've got something to drive, and I am not getting ready to go that far upside down on another car, and absolutely will I not have my daughter to cosign."

Within a week of the Kia's engine seizing, not only had I found myself something to drive that I paid cash for, but I had also been able to acquire a car for my son; out of my tax refund. God had worked it out. Within one week, I had purchased two vehicles.

Nine months later my car was still running well but had started drinking oil. I was adding oil in, knew it needed it because I could hear the valves ticking; but I could not see where the oil was going. There was not a spill on the ground or a trail in the street. The hiccup with the Kia's engine had caused me to buy the Dodge Spirit, that later had the oil leak. The same oil leak; that led me to meet the love of my life.

It is always bigger than you think. Three months into dating him (my heart), the papers came; Kia was honoring the Engine Repair.

THE BURNT CAKE

THE ENGINE ON MY KIA HAD SEIZED AND LEFT US IN A REAL predicament. My family and I were already balancing the shortage of vehicles before it went out. Thank God, my children always worked it out with me; not complaining. Now that the Kia was down and they did not want to fix it, this was more trouble.

When each child turned sixteen, I purchased them a car. My daughter was the first and she did well in school; so, I was eager to get her some wheels. Not so much that she asked but, because she could help; by running errands and getting her brothers back and forth. My daughter had also been the child, on more than one occasion; to volunteer herself to watch the boys and stop my tears.

The first time she did it; I was on a 90-day probationary period for a new job and could not call out. She was home from school sick, and her brother was too. I was crying because I did not want to jeopardize my job and I also had never left them alone while sick. She quickly responded, "Momma, I'll watch him, the most he'll probably do is sleep and if he gets worse, I'll call you." "Are you sure?" I asked. She said, "Yes."

The second time Jolie volunteered, summer was approaching, and I was trying to figure out how I could afford childcare for them all; on the little money I made. I often hid my world from my children, but like myself; my daughter is intuitive. She asked, "What was wrong?" I explained, "That I didn't make enough money to pay for their Summer care," and she volunteered. "Momma, I'll watch the boys," and she did; year after year.

I tried to be fair with my children; I was not going to do more for one than the other. However, the value of your car depended on your behavior, grades, and what you desired in a vehicle. Ethan was the next in line; he has a heart of gold and will give you his last. He wanted a fixer upper sort of car; one he could alter this way or that. He was given a car, much different than Jolie's, but it was still a car.

The baby boy was different. Solomon had been sick, and I had lost the great paying job; so, when he turned sixteen, I was devastated; I cried and cried. No matter how much he said, "It's okay Momma," my heart was broken that I could not do the same for him. When he turned seventeen, again I could not give him a car, and the tears secretly fell.

I say all that to tell you, the plan before the Kia died was to purchase Solomon a car; almost two years from when I felt he should have gotten it. However, the Kia dying threw a curve in those plans. My youngest child is compassionate and when I started running a newspaper route to help pay the bills; he was recovering from his illness. Since he was homeschooled, and we could control his schedule; he offered to ride with me at night.

We would laugh and talk, throw newspapers; while listening to our favorites of country music. Solomon also helped clean offices, before school and when he returned to a regular school routine. So, I wanted to get him a car. I had to continue making payments on the Kia even though it would not move. I did not want a second car payment in a new vehicle; on top of the payment for the Kia. I was in a mess, but I sent up a prayer. "God, it's me," as I often said. "Please help me find an older car, that I can buy straight out for about $700.00, that some elderly person had with low miles and has been well taken care of." I thanked God in advance.

I had filed my taxes and was awaiting a decent refund. If I could find me something to drive and pay cash for it, I would have enough to also help Solomon get a car. I let my family know to keep their eyes out for me some wheels.

My sister was making a cake for my aunts' birthday. Our cousin had ordered it. On the morning my cousin was to pick up the cake; my sister had said, she would deliver it instead; not letting her know, the cake had burnt slightly while baking. My sister re-made and delivered the desert. In route to transport the sugary concoction, she saw a car sitting in someone's yard, with a price marked $700.00. Thea said the car was clean from what she could see. I asked her to go look at it and see what they could find out. If it was good; I would come down and bring the money.

Thea and my mom went to inspect the ride and called back with excellent news. The guy had just put the car out. His parents were the second owners. He said, "His dad had bought the car from one of his friends." "The original owner had kept it so clean; to the point that he would put socks on the foot pedals."

His parents purchased it, but now his dad was deceased; and his mom no longer drove it. He stated, he pulled it out from under the carport and cleaned it off that same morning. It needed a battery that he had just purchased. It had 87,000 original miles and was clean as a whistle. The only flaw: the radio did not work and there was a minor dent on the rear quarter panel on the passenger side. I said, "I'm on my way." I quickly went by the ATM and withdrew the cash. I thanked God for providing the funds to buy my car and for my sister burning the cake. A week later, I also purchased a reliable car for my son.

As my daughter always say, "Look at God, won't he do it!"

THE BLESSINGS DURING COVID 19 (CORONAVIRUS)

THE WORLD AS WE KNEW IT, SEEMED TO CHANGE OVERNIGHT IN 2020. American citizens watched in shock; while news feeds ran across the television with information that China was battling some disease that was killing people and it was highly contagious. By late February 2020, Coronavirus/Covid had made it to the United States.

In no time at all, people in all Fifty States of the United States with the exception to essential workers were confined to their homes. Stores were closed, people were out of work, and fear of dying of this horrible illness was rampant. The broadcast stations were bombarded with reports of cases and deaths of people of all ages due to Covid.

The government sent out stimulus checks to help people bridge the gap of being out of work. Unemployment benefits were available, and millions took advantage of them. In a few short days, there was also no school and parents had to balance becoming a teacher to their children; while working from home and face mask had become mandatory.

Covid was devastating. Alcohol sales were through the roof and domestic violence was on the rise. I saw God immediately in Covid and quickly realized He was going to use this as an opportunity to make people better. Before Covid, people were taking lives for granted; by simply existing. Parents were always on the go and did not invest time with their families. Covid shut it all down; even the church. (What?) Yes, people could not even attend church.

It was no longer an option to pick up dinner or dine out. Suddenly, the world had to cook from home. Meals had to be prepared; not purchased. This resulted in quality time spent at home. Conversations over dinner opened a new awareness of how to be together as a family unit.

Finances were horribly affected. With no work and no income coming in; people were forced to oversee their money more effectively and to reset their priorities without spending so freely.

However, Covid did bless some people in their businesses; mine included. As the world sat confined to their homes, looking at their walls; they started getting decorating ideas. In no time, my cleaning and painting business sales soared; and I was swamped.

Covid also caused people to become more creative and to start doing things they really wanted to do. People lost weight physically, mentally, and spiritually. Individuals decided to start businesses, developed new hobbies, found out that home was something they had missed or that this relationship I am in is toxic and I do not want to do it anymore. Yes, Covid created divorces, but on the upside babies and even new romance.

Although covid caused many deaths; it also changed people's lives for the better. Even with death; people became more aware of life being short and to value the current moment and not take it for granted. Please understand, losing anyone to death is devastating and my heart weeps for you.

However, if Covid brought awareness to you in any of the above-mentioned areas, then Covid, although it seems harsh, was a blessing. *That what does not kill you, makes you stronger.* If you are reading this; you are a survivor of Coronavirus, Covid. Whether you caught the virus, or just suffered the effects; the fact you are still alive, lets you know God has you here for a purpose. You were created for something valuable and there is a need for you to manifest your gift. So live, surround yourself with those who can motivate you to become the best version of you. Stay true to you and look within; asking yourself, am I living my best life? If the answer is no, then get to it, you have been given a second chance to get it right! Stop existing and begin living.

THANK GOD I
CONTRACTED COVID!

Y ES, THE TITLE OF THIS CHAPTER IS, "THANK GOD I CONTRACTED Covid!" What in the world? You are probably wondering, did she just say that; Covid, this deadly disease that is killing the young and the old and you are thanking God that you caught it?

Well, first let me say this, I knew that I would. To be able to write this book "God is in your Mess," every chapter is a first-hand experience; a testimony. At this time, it's 2023 and Covid occurred within the last few years, so yes, I needed to include a chapter of the pandemic. I just did not know when or how severe my symptoms would be but felt assured I would survive it. I believed I had work to do for God that was not finished yet.

The world at this point was turned upside down as Covid was in full force and the medical labs were trying desperately to find a vaccine. Somethings were returning to a partial state of being normal, like food establishments were open for pick up but, mask were still mandatory. Other businesses had closed permanently. My full-time job was working overtime, as we were considered essential workers and so was my personal business. Yes, I was blessed.

The painting side of my work had a fourteen to twenty-one day waiting period. I was painting before work, on my days off, and weekends. I was getting more customers and loved it. Word of mouth was traveling, and my pockets felt nice. There is no better advertisement than positive referrals.

I had been at a customer's home painting his 18-foot-high accent wall and balcony area. The gentleman was genuinely nice, but difficult to complete, as he often changed colors once it was on the wall. I am not complaining; it just required additional time and planning. He paid for each color change.

He was easy to talk to and we shared laughs while I was working. I had been painting in his home the day before and when I returned to complete the work the following day, he responded, "You are going to hate me, but this is too bright!"

Somehow in my gut, I knew he was going to have an issue. I made a color suggestion based on another room he liked and placed the sample on the wall. Yippee, he loved the idea. We went out to buy more paint and the transformation began. Since he was outdoors working, and I was painting inside up high on the ladder; I removed my mask. It is not uncommon for me to get too hot when I paint near the ceiling; as heat rises.

Soon a lady came by to visit him; with her sons. They had been there for a while and one of her sons had slept during the time they were there. Since I was up in the air on the ladder; I felt safe. However, later one of her sons became fascinated with my painting and came closer; asking questions. He seemed fine, but at one point he was so close, that I thought, "Boy, I should have my mask on, maybe I'll be okay." (The whisper of the Holy Spirit)

I got home and the next day the gentleman I had been painting called. Boom, the magic words came out of his mouth. The lady that was there started running a fever and went to the ER, testing positive for Covid. "Ok, I said, thanks for letting me know." I immediately went into quarantine mode. I contacted all my customers explaining that I had been exposed, and I would be quarantined as a precaution.

One of the people I contacted was a new customer. I had only spoken with him by phone for his initial consultation. I sent him a text explaining that I had been exposed and that I was incredibly careful with my customers and would be in quarantine for a few weeks. I said, "I hope you understand." He responded, "Yes and take care."

Two days later, this same gentleman texted me to see how I was doing. I thought, that is odd, I do not know him, and brushed it off, as he was just being nice. I responded, "Very well, very little symptoms, I'm good." He then said, "Remember to get some rest and take care of you." Again, I thought, that is nice; unusual but nice.

Two days after that text, I received a phone call from him. "Hey Lady, I know you're quarantined, and your kids probably are too; do you need me to bring you anything?" "I know you don't know me like that, but I'll be happy to bring you whatever."

I thanked him, and said, "No I'm good, my daughter lives close by and she brings stuff and so does my mom and sister, but I appreciate it." He said, "Sure," and we ended the call.

The next week, he sent a text saying, "I really like your spirit," and I responded, "I think you have a cool vibe too." Although our calls were business related; we always talked a little more. On another day, he called to check on me and to see how I was doing. He was always genuine and would end each call with something like; make sure you take care of you.

When I told him, I was coming out of quarantine and would get him on the books as soon as possible, he responded, "I am sure you are behind on your other customers by now, not to worry, I will find something for you to do, take care of them first." Boy, that was odd, not only was he nice, but he was considerate.

Each conversation with him would be polite and about business, but it was something about him that intrigued me. There were even moments I could be going down the road and wondering to myself what he was doing and within moments; he would call. It was the most unusual thing; we would laugh and talk for minutes at a time. The conversation was always comfortable, like that of old friends.

Then my car started drinking oil. I was putting it in, but I could not see where it was leaking out. I called my cousin to see if he could look at it, but he did not answer. Within minutes, this same guy texted me, "Hey lady, just checking on you, I haven't spoken to you in a while." I said, "I'm good," and in that moment, I remembered he worked on cars as a side hustle, (another example of how the Holy Spirit may work) so I said, "I may need you to check out my car."

He did not respond right away, and I decided to call him. He had asked me before to call him sometime, but I had not. Quickly, he answered, and I asked if he had gotten the message I sent about him checking my car. He said, "That's your main car, right?" I said, "Yes." "This is the one you use for business?" Again, I responded "Yes." "Bring it down then, "he said. I said, "I don't want to inconvenience you, as you weren't planning to mess with my car today." He said, "No, no, to bring it on down." I said, "Ok," and told him about how long it would be for me to get there. He said, "No problem."

I went just like I was; not fixing up or anything. I had my business work clothes on; a pair of jeans, a business t-shirt, and a business hoodie with sneakers. I knew he was interested because he had mentioned that he heard I was single, and he liked my spirit. In route, I spoke to God, saying, "If this guy is really interested, he will ask me to remove my mask so he can see my face. All this time, we had never met, only short conversations about business by phone and text.

Within moments of me pulling in, he came out and I said to myself, "He's kind of cute." I quickly checked him out before he put on his mask. Immediately he began investigating the car; while making polite conversation. "Could you do me a favor?" he asked, and I responded "Yes," (but in my mind I was thinking I don't know you) then he said it, "Could you remove your mask so I can see your face? I dropped the loop from my ear on one side; looked at him and smiled. He responded, "Just like I thought, absolutely beautiful."

To make a long story short, he fixed my car, asked me on a date, and we are still together 18 months later. He is my heart and the love of my life. Yes, I thank God for Covid. If God had not slowed me down; with the illness, I would not have noticed him.

THE UNKNOWING

THIS CHAPTER IS PAINFUL; TEARS ARE CRESTING IN MY EYES AND my chest heaves in anguish. My breath is weary, as my sniffles come and go. I am moments away from going into a full-blown crying spell. As I try to get this chapter down on paper; I can no longer control my emotions and the tears freely flow. This hurts!

See, authoring this book is not always easy as some of the chapters are uncomfortable to endure. Because God leads me, I cannot write about them until I have experienced it. There is no harder aching than the one of being in love with someone, and they in turn love you the same; you can see it in their eyes, but because of their previous relationships and their pain; they tuck tail and run. This hurts you to your core because you do not understand.

That saying of loving someone through their pain; ooh, that is not easy, when they figuratively fight you on it. To protect themselves from possible heartache; they push you away because they are falling for you, and it scares them. They openly tell you they love you and you know it. You can tell by the way they treat you, but they said they thought they were ready for you but found out they are not. They even say, if God would just confirm its okay, but in the same breath they say; they can't hear God, He is not talking. In your gut, you know they are telling you the truth; not only can you see it in their eyes, but you can also feel it. It is a mess.

This is the same relationship that God confirmed to you that He sent it him, but understanding how God works in your mess; sometimes is not how you see it. Did God put the two of you together? Yes! So, why aren't the two of you sunshine and rainbows? It is bigger than you think. Sometimes, God being in your stuff is as my dad says; "It's a matter of trust."

God knows the plans He has for you (Jeremiah 29:11). Occasionally, He will give you a glimpse into your future, but there are things you need to work on before you are ready. When God brings two people together, it is a God ordained relationship; meaning He arranged for you to be one another's mate for life to fulfil His purpose.

> For I know the plans I have for you," declares the Lord,
> "plans to prosper you and not to harm you, plans to
> give you hope and a future. (Jeremiah 29:11 NIV)

What am I honestly saying to you? God can send you the Right One at the Wrong Time. He can confirm that this is your person, but timing may be off. According to *Stephan Speaks, YouTube video titled "HE WAS SENT FOR YOU!"* There are 5 *reasons Why GOD Will Send You the RIGHT MAN at the Wrong Time."* (Please refer to the video for the exact reasons) An example could be, if there was pain from a previous relationship, then that pain must be dealt with; otherwise, it is like bringing the old person into the new relationship and that is not fair to either party.

Or, a person has been alone for so long, that even in the best of relationships; they will not honor themselves by speaking up if something is uncomfortable. Even as I write these words on paper, I am speaking to my own situation; myself. To author a book that will honor God, He assists me in the writing process; giving me insight. Therefore, I must trust Him even when I do not understand; even if it hurts. (Proverbs 3:5-6)

> Trust in the Lord with all your heart and lean not on your
> own understanding; ⁶ in all your ways submit to him, and
> he will make your path straight. (Proverbs 3:5-6 NIV)

The words that I have learned and studied in the past few months are like medicine to my soul. To not act emotionally, as pain often comes with emotions. If we respond by our feelings, we may not act appropriately. Heartache and tears during a moment like this can sometimes cause you to not hear what is really being said.

> So, I tell you this, and insist on it in the Lord, that you must no
> longer live as the Gentiles do, in the futility of their thinking. ¹⁸

They are darkened in their understanding and separated from the life of God because of the ignorance that is in them due to the hardening of their hearts. [19] Having lost all sensitivity, they have given themselves over to sensuality so as to indulge in every kind of impurity, and they are full of greed. (Ephesians 4:17-19 NIV)

Get rid of all bitterness, rage, and anger, brawling and slander, along with every form of malice. [32] Be kind and compassionate to one another, forgiving each other, just as in Christ God forgave you. (Ephesians 31-32 NIV)

A figuratively wounded and scarred person who is still broken; are not whole. They are like a wounded dog backed into a corner; fearful and dangerous. Although, you approach lovingly and wanting to assist, or be there for them; to get them out you may get bitten. Therefore, when a wounded person knows and acknowledges that they have not dealt with some pain, some bitterness, has some anger, or maybe some closet skeletons they do not want to confront; they are broken. As painful as it is; the bigger picture is they love you enough to not want to hurt you; so, they pull themselves away.

At the same time, one must look within. When this wonderful, magical relationship started, other than the painful moments I had not let go of; I felt complete and whole; confident in myself.

Because I wanted our relationship to grow and prosper; as well has help my man with his pain, I read books, search through scriptures, and listened to sermons. In doing so, guess what? I found out that I too was flawed and wounded. There was pain I had locked away; hidden even from myself. I knew there were some things I needed to work on, but I did not expect this. We all if truth be told, have hidden secrets; closet skeletons that we do not want people to know about. However, those skeletons we do not want to deal with or confront; become luggage or furniture that we take to the next place or in this case the next relationship. When we honestly look at our situation and put on the other person's shoes; is it fair to them? No, it is not.

"Every day that breath is given, is the opportunity to change, be better, try something new." "Don't waste it!" When you can step back, look at your situation, be honest with yourself, and take ownership of your flaws and shortcomings; you grow.

God has remarkable things in store for you, but sometimes He must inflict pain to build us, so we can reach our real potential. Even if that means; He removes someone special. When He is done, you are going to be better and will be in a happier place. A place where your inner light can shine, the magic that radiates through you like a magnet. If you allow God to assist you with this and not become bitter or angry; when God is finished; it will be worth it. As *TD Jakes sermon says, "Bigger than you think!"* God is always moving on your behalf, and He promises to never leave you or forsake you (Hebrews 13:5)

> *Keep your lives free from the love of money and be content with what you have, because God has said, "Never will I leave you; never will I forsake you. (Hebrews 13:5 NIV)*

Taking into consideration the fact that God never leaves us; confirms He is always with us in our storms, our crisis. Therefore, God is in our mess; growing us, helping us to become the person He created us to be. When life happens as it sometimes will, instead of throwing in the towel or giving up; roll up your sleeves, put on your most comfortable clothes and get busy. God, I can promise you; is up to something wonderful in your life. (Romans 8:28) Trust him!

> *And we know that in all things God works for the good of those who love him, who have been called according to his purpose. (Romans 8:28 NIV)*

HONEY THE HOUSE IS ON FIRE!

SUPPER HAD BEEN FINISHED, THE DISHES CLEANED, PUT AWAY, and everyone had gone to bed. No one was stirring around; even though both the kids had laid down late. Suddenly, the doorbell rang, "Ding- Dong." "Was that the doorbell?" Josiah and Thea, both asked each other through drowsy eyes. Then they heard it again. "Ding- Dong," but this time it continued becoming more frequent. "Ding - Dong, Ding - Dong, Ding - Dong." It is roughly 3:30 am, who in the world is ringing the doorbell? Josiah said as he rolled out of the bed, with my sister Thea following close behind.

Down the hall and to the door; with sleep still in their eyes, Josiah opened the door but there was no one there. Not a soul in sight. Thea asked Josiah, "Do I smell smoke?" as Josiah turns around to retreat to bed, he sees a bright orange glow towards the back porch deck area of the house. Although groggy, he quickly assessed that the house was on fire and tells my sister. Still disoriented from being awaken by the doorbell, my sister asks, "Who's house is on fire?" "Ours, he says, wake the kids, we've got to go."

The house was quiet, with no smoke alarms going off as they quickly moved to get everyone out. Within moments the lights went out. Using the kids cell phones as flashlights, they exited out the front door of their home; never once coughing because there was no smoke. There was also no need to wet blankets, as there were no flames.

Once standing in the yard, facing their home, they could see the blaze consuming the roof; while calls were made to 911 reporting the fire and their need for assistance. In no time, the neighbors were coming from everywhere; awakened by the sound of fire trucks and the bright lights. "Do you need anything? they asked, here are blankets to wrap up in and chairs to sit on." A few of the neighbors had only been waved at or briefly spoken to when out in the yard. Please do not hesitate to ask for anything they would say. Others went through their cabinets and pantries for snacks, bottled water, and hand sanitizer. While some made coffee, ordered biscuits, and even cried; thanking God that no one was hurt.

Did anyone say, I saw the house was in flames and rang the doorbell trying to wake you up? Not a soul.

In fact, one neighbor that lives at the beginning of the dead-end street, confirmed that he had been up moving about within his home and would have heard if a car had come down the street; but not a soul. Yet, the doorbell had rung. Normally, a fire in the middle of the night does not end well; however, all four family members walked out; with no smoke in their lungs, no soot on their skin and no burns because they had not battled any flames.

Their lives had been saved; all because of the doorbell, that no one acknowledges that they rang. Only God himself, the lover and protector of His sheep; could have performed such a feat as this. Yes, the home ended up being a total loss, but the most valuable and uniquely designed, one-of-a-kind creations walked out alive.

Once the fire was put out, the walkthrough of the house that provided shelter only hours ago; indicated the roof was completely gone. The windows had been blown out, there was no indication of the original color of the walls and much of the drywall was gone; revealing its basic frame structure. The siding had melted from the heat, as well as every bed had burned; yet all members that dwelled within had survived.

God protected and shielded them, giving them the opportunity to live another day; to complete goals, fulfil dreams, and glorify His name.

Phone calls came in from people that recognized my sister on the news; as well as out of pure compassion. Individuals started sending money, donating food, clothes and even an entire house of furniture. Huge boxes of supplies included: toiletries, wipes, sanitizer, and laptops for the kids that were lost in the fire but needed for their college classes. People made meals, offered shelter, even strangers working construction that morning on the street; reached in their wallets voluntarily to donate. The outpouring of love was tremendous.

Miraculously, the family's photo albums survived the fire; along with a championship baseball ring earned by my nephew and the college diploma of my niece received a few days earlier. Things of importance like wallets, purses, one of the two sets of car keys, as well as three out of four cell phones were also recovered.

There was minor heat damage to both cars, and it would have been more if my niece had not listened to the whisper the day before; deciding to move her car up towards the street.

God performed miracles and wonders in the days the bible was written, and He is still performing them today; my sister and her family are living proof.

WEATHERING THE STORM

SOMETIMES LIFE CAN THROW YOU SOME STUMBLING BLOCKS THAT seem like concrete boulders. Upon impact, they not only knock the wind out of your sails, but they do physical damage. This sort of harm you can heal from, but never quite be the same. As in the fact, that life will never go back to where it was.

Divorce and the loss of someone special like a spouse, parent, child, sibling, or close friend can cause this kind of devastation. These types of hurt do not heal easily and often go un-noticed by family and friends, but God sees all and understands. (Proverbs 15:3)

> *The eyes of the Lord are everywhere, keeping watch on*
> *the wicked and the good. (Proverbs 15:3NIV)*

There is not a single moment or tear you have shed that God has not collected. (Psalm 56:8) Believe it or not God grieves with us. (Psalm 34:18)

> *Record my misery; list my tears on your scroll- are they not on record?*
> *(Psalm 56:8NIV)*

> *The Lord is close to the brokenhearted and saves those who are*
> *crushed in spirit. (Psalm 34:18NIV)*

This example of God being in your mess is taken from myself being on the outside looking into the heart of my love. I watched the pain and devastation of my man tear his heart apart; as he lost those loved ones closest to him. In a little over a years' time, he went from meeting the love of his life

104

to extreme pain and heart break; from the deaths of both parents and other close family members. One by one, they were picked like delicate flowers for the most prized vase that heaven could hold. Talk about things being rough, even the strongest of Christians with this type of back-to-back grief find it hard to go on. For me to love him through it has been rough also; because as close as I was, I still missed the signs.

I wanted to support him through this season but missed the quiet unsaid words. It took long conversations with God to help me read between the lines; realizing that his world was crushed by life moments coming back-to-back. Even after God showed me the grief, he himself did not realize or acknowledge that was what was going on. My deep faith and belief in God, allowed God to show me the pain that others did not see. Not only could I see it, but I also felt it. My spirit wrestled because his spirit wrestled.

I often searched in his eyes; as eyes are the windows to the soul. Life seemed gone; there was darkness there that I just could not reach. He often would say his mind was all over the place and he had difficulty focusing on normal day-to-day tasks. He said, "He could not hear God." He was pulling not only away from me, but also friends and family. The closeness we shared over eighteen months let me know he was not himself; he was not ok. I was not only the love of his life, but his best friend and he was mine. Because I desired to help him so, I started researching how to help those you love with grief. It was in that moment, I discovered he was in full blown grief of the first death, not to mention the second, or even later the third; which took him completely left.

The findings of grief and its symptoms were most alarming when I found a book titled *"Its Ok that you're NOT OK, meeting grief and loss in a Culture that doesn't understand" by Megan Devine*. Every word he had shared over the months of grieving were confirmed: not able to focus, easily irritated, not wanting to be around people, extreme fatigue, a huge desire to protect his heart by refusing to allow people in. (If I do not let them in, I will not lose them to death.) The way he began to work from sunup to sundown was even a symptom of grief. It was his way of healing; keeping his mind busy to alleviate pain. In all honesty, he had begun to just exist in life; not live.

As I write these words, I carefully think of him; not wanting anyone that knows him to think harshly about his actions. There are also moments when I have been conflicted in writing this, because I love him so, (yes, right up to this very moment even though the deaths have separated us; he is still my heart.) I wish to protect him from all pain and suffering. However, GRIEF is real and maybe just maybe, by me expressing his pain, it will help someone recognize their partner or family member is in a crisis.

Grief is not only caused by death, but can be through a job loss, a breakup or even the result of a divorce. Realistically, grief is anything that takes the wind out of your sails. When a person is experiencing this type of hurt by the deaths of those closest to them; they know NOT what they do. They isolate, retreat, withdraw, even attach to a stranger because after a while they just need to feel something; anything. Sorrow does not have an exit date. It can last for weeks, months, even years on end, and most people on the outside looking in cannot see what is happening for the cloudy windows to the soul.

They cannot fathom that this person is still suffering. It never crosses their mind. Because the outside world does not understand; they quickly say, you need to get over it, you need to move on. Never realizing that the person thinks, I know that is what I need to do; however, moving on causes me to forget, and I do not want to forget them. Also, there are days that the simplest of things reminds you of them; like seeing a Krispy Kreme donut sign and this reminds you of the donuts you shared; which brings a flood of tears. Riding down the road that you and they used to travel on often reminds you of them. Smells remind, coffee reminds, washing powders remind; everything reminds you of them.

Going to work, you think is a great idea until you get there and then you cannot wait to leave; so, you can cry while no one is looking. Five minutes alone is a short amount of time, but for someone heartbroken; those three thousand seconds can bring a flood of tears because you have time to think. Yes, you know you should move on, you want to move on; if someone could just tell you where to discard the pain; just tell me how to make it stop. Please, just tell me where to place the pain and I can move on; are *like* their thoughts. It took me a long time to understand, I was grieving too.

It is no wonder that relationships fall apart during a mourning period. Because the other person does not recognize the signs; they quickly start the cycle saying things like, "Well, I am not going to put up with this, when you get your act together, call me." She stopped showing me affection, so I am out, or he is drinking and acting unusual; I am not tolerating this, he must go."

My heart weeps for those that are suffering, and on top of their pain; they lose their partner because they simply did not see the signs.

It is because of how deeply I care for people that I write this chapter. Grief took my love away. I pray daily for him as I can feel his pain; he never realized it. I loved him enough to grieve with him, for him, as well as grieve that which was lost. Even my expressions of heartache, through that of my love, is no comparison to the **EXTREME PAIN** he himself has felt. Because of my faith in God, I hold no anger or resentment. I knew with all my being, that he loved me, but life became too hard for him to bear.

Afterall, if you put yourself in his shoes, and try to understand this sort of heartache, there is no telling what you; too may do. In all reality, your mind cannot grasp this, even with your best effort, you cannot. On top of that, grief has no quick fix, everyone handles it differently, but I am so grateful that God showed me his pain, and often spoke to me saying, do not forget he is grieving.

It has been months and I still love him just as much. I also still do not have any anger or bitterness towards him, because even in the bible Jesus said, forgive them for they know not what they do. (Luke 23:34) Not to mention how many times we are to forgive. (Matthew 18:21-22)

Jesus said, "Father, forgive them, for they do not know what they are doing. "And they divided up his clothes by casting lots. (Luke 23:34 NIV)

Then Peter came to Jesus and asked, "Lord, how many times shall I forgive my brother or sister who sins against me? Up to seven times?" [22] Jesus answered, "I tell you, not seven times, but seventy-seven times. (Matthew 18:21-23NIV)

This is a side note, please, please, I beg you; if you love your person and see this sort of grief, urge them to get help. Love them enough to not give up on them. It will take time, but I pray for you, that they will not withdraw completely from you. Invest in the book immediately or research the stages of grief when death comes, so that you can recognize the words that they say.

The death of one person can be traumatic alone but combine back-to-back or even worst; loose multiple members at the same time and one just checks out of life. Their emotional tank is on fumes, and they cannot bear one more thing. They may talk of not wanting to exist anymore and in the same breath never are suicidal, but at the same time another person could be. You MUST read between the lines and adjust quickly and accordingly.

Yes, those mourning need time alone to release their feelings, but be close enough to check in; if nothing more than to say I will be right here whenever you need me even if that means we share time and space without saying a word. This could mean sleeping in different beds for a moment; occupying different rooms in the house. **And for women, hint, hint: when a man says he is ok; he is not. He wants you to care enough to reach him in his pain; not by questioning but comfort.** A hand to his face, a hug or a kiss to the cheek assuring him you understand; even when you may not. Men do not express themselves the same as women.

Pray for them and please understand that some types of grief needs therapy, and that it is ok to need a therapist. The truth is everyone could use assistance; as we all have some form of dysfunction in our lives, no matter what lifestyle we come from. If you were abandoned during grief of a loved one, it is called Disenfranchised Grief and happens more than we know. There is also special assistance for you; to heal and adjust.

Please DO NOT take grief lightly; as it's simple and you should just get over it. If we live long enough; the tables will turn, and you may find yourself to be the one grieving. God's passion and love for us in life is huge and in death as well.

***Below you will find scriptures and sermons to offer encouragement in times of death and grief.

"The Lord is close to the brokenhearted and saves those
who are crushed in spirit (Psalm 34:18 NIV)

"Blessed are those who mourn, for they will
be comforted. (Matthew 5:4 NIV)

'He will wipe every from their eyes. There will be no more
death' or mourning or crying, or pain, for the old order
of things has passed away." (Revelation 21:4 NIV)

Blessed are you who hunger now, for you will be satisfied. Blessed are you who weep now, for you will laugh. (Luke 6:21 NIV)

Peace I leave with you, my peace I give you. I do not give to you as the world gives. Do not let your hearts be troubled and do not be afraid. (John 14:27NIV)

Sermons on YouTube

TD Jakes: Heart Full of Grief and a Horn Full of Oil
Steven Furtick: God Can Handle Your Broken Heart
Don't Let Grief Overtake Your View
The Moody Church: Grieving Loss It's Ok To Not Be Okay
Pastor Keion Henderson: Coping with Collapse
Tony Evans: How to Live and Cope With Loss in Your Life
Dr. Charles Stanley: The Courage to Keep Going

"CRAZY FAITH !!!"

I READ ALL THE TIME. VERY RARELY DOES ONE CATCH ME WITHOUT a book. Funny thing is in school I hated to read. In fact, I would cheat at reading on class assignments; by reading the first chapters, skipping to the middle, read the last, and guess what happened in between.

However, if you put the right subject or content in any person's hands; they will read. Smut, as old folks say, opened the door to my love of reading. I am grateful that I developed it because reading has taken me on vacation in my mind; as I visualized the words on the page.

It created an outlet; providing a way to relax and unwind. In my later years as my genres have changed, reading has helped me grow as a person. During my injury to healing state, I have had more than plenty of time to do nothing but read. It does not take long to read a book during a 12-hour work shift; confined to the light duty area of a computer lab.

I started ordering books online to keep me busy, but soon ran out of them and had to resort to shopping locally. Three days, back-to-back on a work shift can cause one to deplete their stock of reading material quickly. Thankfully, there are still stores that carry books in house. There are online materials called eBooks, but I am old school and prefer one in my hands that I can flip through its pages.

On one of these shopping excursions, my hands landed on a book titled, *"Crazy Faith: It's Only Crazy Until It Happens," by Michael Todd*. He is the pastor of Transformation Church in Tulsa, OK. "Crazy Faith" was an extremely easy book to read and very informative.

Shortly after reading this book, my daughter Jolie was struggling with one of her classes. She was studying to obtain her masters in Midwifery. This class was the last one she needed to graduate.

Jolie is very studious and has accomplished a lot. I know what she is capable of, however, this course had her weighing her options of dropping the class, retaking it later, or sticking it out. Because my daughter and I are close, she discussed her dilemma with me by phone; covering all the options.

> Option One: continue with the class and possibly not be able to pull her grade up; resulting in the need to retake the course.

> Option Two: drop the class now, so it does not hurt her GPA (grade point average) and retake the class when it is next offered.

> Option Three: if you drop the class and wait; financially will you be able to maintain? For her to do this program, she had to stop working to free up time for the Clinical portion of the course.

> Option Four: worst case scenario if she continued and failed, what the result would be?

I assured her no matter what her choice was, I would support her decision and we completed the call. Within moments, I felt a nudge to encourage her (The whisper of The Holy Spirit). I called her back and said, "You can do whatever you want, but why not have Crazy Faith?" I told her to talk with God and ask Him to help her pass the class. I said, "Tell God, I am going to put the work in by studying on this end; if He will do the rest." I said again, "To have Crazy Faith, Crazy Faith!"

A few days later, she was studying for a test; an indication that she was going for it. We would talk often; this was approximately six weeks before her graduation date. Anytime school and classes would come up in conversation, I would remind her to have "Crazy Faith"; always putting emphasis on the words. In no time, her test scores were improving. If I spoke with her on a day she was going to have an exam, or I was aware of her test date; I would spiritually fast by turning down my plate until she finished her test. Soon her high-test scores had increased her GPA to a passing grade.

Her graduation date was within a week, and we had made plans to attend; even though she was graduating out of the state. I asked, "Have you ordered your cap and gown yet?" She responded, "No, I haven't because there is one more test I have to pass." So, I asked her if I could step on her toes. Reluctantly, she said, "Yes." I call her Sweet Pea, and so I said, "Sweet Pea, that's not 'Crazy Faith;' waiting until you pass." "Crazy Faith is ordering the gown, knowing you will pass; and we will hear them jack your name up when you walk across that stage. (Jolie is her nick name not her birth name of Joleineque.) She said, "Ok ma, I'm ordering it now." Five days later, my Sweet Pea walked across that stage to get draped in her master's apparel. On top of her cap were the words, CRAZY FAITH got me here.

(Her cap brought tears then, and even now when I read back over the chapters while correcting this book; the tears flow. Happy Tears! God has been so incredibly good to me. I had a WOW moment of reflection, while editing and proofing these pages; I wrote and shared, to inspire others to believe and have faith, not realizing my own words, given by God would bless me too.

Each chapter reminded me of the awesomeness of God and that He cannot be put in a box. God is too Big, too wonderful, too loving, too forgiving, too kind, too compassionate, and His ways are not like our ways. I find it difficult to think of God and remain without emotion. He, (God) is wonderful to me! I apologize for deviating momentarily from the flow of this book; I just had to say, how He makes me feel; Absolutely Loved and Cared For in a manner most may not understand, but it's ok.

Just as I had advised my daughter to have "Crazy Faith", I have inspired others to have "Crazy Faith" too. I was moved within our department to help a lady on the job named Ruth. We knew and recognized each other by face but had never worked together; until this day. While waiting for the driver to move the materials, Ms. Ruth asked me about my kids and specifically what they did for a living. Always the proud mom, I told her my daughter was a Labor and Delivery nurse who just got her masters in Midwifery. My middle son, Ethan, went to college to do Collision and Body work and my baby son, Solomon works in Construction. I told her just last weekend we had went to my daughter's graduation and that she almost quit on the tail end because her grades were low.

I heard "the whisper" to keep talking about my daughter. I told her that I advised my daughter to have "Crazy Faith"; her putting in the work by studying and asking God to work on His end to help her pass.

Ms. Ruth, lit up like a Christmas tree. She said, her daughter Jennifer was also struggling and was considering quitting one of her classes that was needed to get her Masters. When she said this, I explained in detail the message I had said to my daughter and showed her a picture of my daughter with her cap that said, "CRAZY FAITH got me here." She decided she was going to tell her daughter to do the same thing.

As soon as this conversation stopped; I was requested to work somewhere else. Before I left I told her, "It was meant for us to have this talk; as I have only been over here about twenty minutes." "How odd was it, that of all the questions you could have asked, it brought up my daughter's Crazy Faith testimony." "It is not coincidental that your daughter is struggling with the same thing." "Tell Jennifer, God has already worked it out; it is done!" Ms. Ruth was overjoyed with excitement.

Periodically, in the weeks following that conversation, she would show me Jennifer's grades and how she was pulling up her scores too. Just like I said, Jennifer passed her class in late October; about a month after we had spoken. In the middle of the floor, like two wild women; we danced in joy as to what God had done.

In life and in different circumstances, we must apply Faith. Faith is the action that you combine with what you are hoping for. Faith cannot work without hope; as well as hope cannot work without Faith. Together they are amazing. A fitting example of this is in this quote. *"Hope is praying for rain, but faith is bringing the umbrella (in anticipation that it will rain.) author unknown.*

Depending on your current mindset, combined with the situation; will determine the quantity of your faith. Always remember, Mustard Seed faith is all you need. In case you are unsure how much that is; (Matthew 17:20) a mustard seed, is smaller than the period (.) at the end of this sentence; which is not much.

He replied, "Because you have so little faith. Truly I tell you,
if you have faith as small as a mustard seed, you can say to
this mountain, 'Move from here to there,' and it will move.
Nothing will be impossible for you." (Matthew17:20-21 NIV)

You can enhance that faith; as my love once said to me: "If you have mustard seed faith and I have mustard seed faith, that creates watermelon seed faith, and a watermelon seed is big enough to choke on." In other words, "CRAZY FAITH", because the bible says where two or more agree, God will be in the midst. (Matthew 18: 19-20)

"Again, truly I tell you that if two of you on earth agree
about anything they ask for, it will be done for them by my
Father in heaven.²⁰ For where two or three gather in my
name, there am I with them." (Matthew 18; 19-20 NIV)

A WILDERNESS SEASON

THIS CHAPTER IS FOR THE PERSON THAT ALREADY HAS A CLOSE relationship with God. However, it will prove valuable to those building a bond with Him as well; a reminder for when it is your season of **growing** Faith. Remember, to build or grow your faith, it MUST be tested. There is no other way to get there.

> *Dear friends, do not be surprised at the fiery ordeal that has come on you to test you, as though something strange were happening to you. [13] But rejoice inasmuch as you participate in the sufferings of Christ, so that you maybe overjoyed when his glory is revealed. (1Peter 4:12-13 NIV)*

By this time, you and God have had conversations and built a rapport. God knows your voice. (John 10:27) Yet there are periods of time in which God may seem like He is not talking. You may pray and pray, and God is not telling you anything. It is not that He has left you, as God would never go against His word; His promises. (Deuteronomy 31:6).

> *My sheep listen to my voice; I know them, and they follow me. (John 10:27NIV)*

> *Be strong and courageous. Do not be afraid or terrified because of them, for the Lord your God goes with you; he will never leave you nor forsake you." (Deuteronomy 31:6 NIV)*

However, He will go silent. If you do not believe me, look at Noah in the book of Genesis (chapter 6 &7). God gave instructions to Noah on how to build the ark; what materials to use, spoke about the animals, and the use of the ark when the rains came. It was estimated that based on Noah's age, and his children's ages, it took close to 120 years to build the ark. During this time God said little to Noah. Also, God did not speak for over 400 years between the Old Testament and the New Testament. This is a valuable lesson God wanted us to learn; sometimes we need to be quiet and not speak. (Ecclesiates3:7)

> O God do not remain silent; do not turn a deaf ear,
> do not stand aloof, O God. (Psalm 83:1 NIV)

> To you, Lord, I call; you are my Rock, do not turn a
> deaf ear to me. For if you remain silent, I will be like
> those who go down to the pit. (Psalm 28:1)

> "Whom have you so dreaded and feared that you have
> not been true to me, and have neither remembered me
> nor taken this to heart? Is it not because I have long been
> silent that you do not fear me? (Isaiah 57:11 NIV)

> A time to tear and a time to mend, a time to be silent
> and a time to speak (Ecclesiastes 3:7 NIV)

There are moments in life that God will be in communication with you, but you must be at a still place. This can be extremely difficult. It seems that no matter what you try, things are not moving. He has given you partial instructions but has not explained what is going on. Guess what, He does not have to. Afterall, He is God. Who are you going to complain to? God, for lack of a better word in plain language is: Top Dawg, The Head Honcho, The CEO, The Supreme Creator. There is no one bigger than Him.

> God said to Moses, "I AM WHO I AM. This is what you say to
> the Israelites: 'I AM has sent me to you." (Exodus 3:14 NIV)

> For in him all things were created: things in heaven and on
> earth, visible and invisible, whether thrones or powers or

rulers or authorities; all things have been created through
him and for him. [17] *He is before all things, and in him*
all things hold together. (Colossians1:16-17 NIV)

In the beginning was the Word, and the Word was with
God, and the Word was God. (John 1:1 NIV)

These times are seasons of growth and character development. They are to build your faith; a spiritual test of your trust in God. Will you continue to speak with Him? Will you pray without ceasing, even if it hurts? Will you, during your tears, cry out to God, I need you; my world is out of sorts. Will you still pray if He does not answer? Will you seek Him and follow Him when you have no idea where you are going?

There are even periods where, God gave you a little bit of information/instructions; without the whole picture to see if you will do as He asked? "I am going to show you somethings but stay;" is a phrase God may say to you. Your mind races and attempts to process what was said. I am going to show you something(s); what things? When you say stay; what do you mean stay? Stay in this position? Stay supportive? Stay where? You will even find yourself feeling ridiculous; looking up the definition of the word stay.

When God goes silent in your stay, you will over time think; surely this is not what He meant; this hurts. In your mind you believe there must be a different definition and you go back to Websters to try and understand.

Your entire life, at this point, is out of your control. The job is off, you feel out of balance, and you cannot seem to progress, or the business is on hold. Your heart is broken, and you want to flee, but God said, stay. Stay for what, am I going to get a promotion? When you said stay; did you mean in that relationship that went off the deep end, or do you mean stay here; as in the location? Am I staying because my better will be here? What I saw; was that what you meant for me to see? What are you showing me? God, I do not understand and guess what; He is not talking.

You know that God is working, because He has done this before, but nothing on this level. Again, God is not responding. You search sermons, listen to songs, pray, meditate, fast and not one word.

You go back and read the instructions, looking closely; did I miss something? What is it? The tears flood your world as you realize; I am not in control of anything, but everything is a miss. Your heart hurts, the job is in stuck mode, the money is beyond funny, but you know God. You remember His words; I am working it out for your good. (Romans 8:28)

> And we know that in all things God works for the
> good of those who love him, who have been called
> according to his purpose. (Romans 8:28 NIV)

It sounds good, but how are you working it out? You cannot see anything; in fact, it is getting worse. Is this what you are going to show me? Man, you thought; what you saw was bad until the bad got even worse. Add in that things are wrong in your physical house: the plumbing is off, everything is breaking, you and the family are fighting over stuff, the kids are acting up and you are one thread from losing your mind; but your faith says, I got to trust God.

It is overwhelming! What started off as days, has now gone into months, and you are reminding yourself; God said, "He wouldn't leave me nor forsake me." I know God is up to something but, what? On top of that, now there are car troubles. You feel like you are about to break; if not physically, mentally, and definitely spiritually. You pray more and more, but do not really know what to pray for; nothing seems to be moving. (Romans 8:26-27)

> In the same way, the Spirit helps us in our weakness. We do not
> know what we ought to pray for, but the Spirit himself intercedes
> for us through wordless groans. [27] And he who searches our hearts
> knows the mind of the Spirit, because the Spirit intercedes for God's
> people in accordance with the will of God. (Romans 8:26-27 NIV)

Again, you pull out the instructions and read; I must be missing something. So, you research the spiritual meaning of the word stay.

> He says, "Be still, and know that I am God; I will be exalted among
> the nations, I will be exalted in the earth." (Psalm 46:10 NIV)

> Be strong and take heart, all you who hope
> in the Lord. (Psalm 31:24 NIV)

You my dear, at this point are grasping at straws; you are in a wilderness season. God is testing you and has you in training. Training you for what?

The very gift God gave you, confirmed it was yours; He has now taken away. You do not understand, and God is not talking. You know God is listening, you know He is there, and more time goes by.

These are the moments that cause even the strongest of believers to shed tears, be frustrated, have moments of doubt, restless nights, more tears and in the same breath; know what you are going through is for your good. You cannot see it. You do not know what is happening. It is not letting up; so, you begin saying, "God, you've been too good to me, for me not to trust you." "I have got to trust you, even when it hurts." You may even find yourself saying, "God I do not like this. "Whatever you are working on God, maybe I don't...," shoot, you cannot even finish that sentence; because you know God. He can always bless you; better than you could imagine. You are also aware; that this season, this wilderness period will not last always. God will see you through it.

Has anyone had a wilderness season? Have you felt you were at a breaking point? Maybe this is where you are right now. Please read this chapter with an open mind; understanding God knows best. Remember that God sits high and looks low. He is all seeing and all knowing. He is in your past, your present and your future; all at the same time. God created you. He selected your parents before you were born; to fulfill your purpose in life. God created the end first, then the beginning. Therefore, He knows how wonderful you are going to be, He must move you to get it!

Dr. Myles Munroe says in a book titled, "*A Woman of Purpose and Power*" "Everything that God has made in this life has a purpose." "He made us the way we are for His purposes and for our benefit and He begins with a finished product in mind." Another book that helps with this is "*The Purpose Driven life,*" *written by a Christian Pastor named Rick Warren,* that references most of that. A lot of ministers call this a wilderness season, I prefer to say, "When God throws you a curve."

I have known of God and was taught to believe in Him; for as long as I can remember. As little children, my sister and I sat on church pews with doodle pads while my mom or grandparents listened to sermons. Even when I did not understand the message, too little to care, church was a part of regular life. My grandparents helped my mom raise us. Unlike parents of today, who give their children options, as to whether they want to go to church or not; we were (termed) Drug Babies. Drug babies are not addicted to drugs, they are drug to church, Sunday school, church meetings, choir rehearsal, trustee meetings, Deacon & Deaconess meetings, and choir anniversaries.

If any event was happening at church, you as a child would be in tow; drugged back and forth, in and out of church. Sundays, you may have felt like you were in church all day. It would start first thing in the morning with Sunday school, (the teaching part of the bible); followed by the service that consisted of prayers, biblical readings, a sermon performed by someone in the pulpit, the choir would sing songs, and service would finally end.

Church would be dismissed long enough to have Sunday dinner with family; which may consist of: Golden Fried Chicken, creamed potatoes and gravy, potato salad, beans, macaroni and cheese, greens, yams, dinner rolls, sweet tea, Kool aid, or lemonade. (The old-fashioned kind made from real lemons.) Not to mention dessert: coconut pie, sweet potato pie, rice pudding, a pound cake, chocolate cake, even fried pies. Sunday dinner was not Sunday dinner without dessert.

As kids, we would run and play a while; then get drugged back to church for a choir anniversary or a second service. Yes, we got tired but what was a child to do; nothing but whine and endure. Even with that, you had better not whine too much, because that would not go over well.

I remember words often said to kids that whined at church, "Keep on and I'll give you something to whine for." Other words quoted by drugged babies include, "Oh you're going to church, or you can take a whipping and still go to church." Regardless, you were going to church. There are even people that will tell you, they may have partied the night before, came in late or early morning intoxicated, and they had still better be in church and on time.

I say all that to say; back in the day (even sometimes now) children that are raised up in church, learned of who God is by being in the church house. Sunday after Sunday whether doodling, playing with baby dolls, or cars; eventually something would spark your interest to listen.

Either, the preacher got loud, the choir sang a song that you liked, or someone on your row got the Holy Spirit and started shouting. No matter what, I do not know of anyone that was brought up in church that does not know God. They may choose not to believe in God, but in an out of church as children; you learn who God is and hopefully, decide you want a personal relationship with Him for yourself.

My only regret in life is I wish I had accepted Christ /God into my world earlier. I was around nineteen when I did. I know I used to stress my Grandma out, because she would emphasize that we needed to be saved. The term saved means to invite Christ into your life by verbally acknowledging that Jesus died on the cross and rose three days later for our sins. According to the bible, children will automatically go to heaven if they unknowingly sin, but once you are old enough to know right from wrong; your actions have consequences. Older generations anticipated this was about the age of 12 or 13.

Often, my Grandmother would mention that my sister and I needed to be saved. I believed that to be a Christian, I had to walk a perfect life. I thought I had to cross every "T" and dot every "I." I knew I could repent of my sins but what good was that if I was going to sin again. Therefore, I would answer my grandma by saying, "God and I have an understanding and there wasn't a need to become a Christian and have to constantly ask for forgiveness." Thinking back on it now, I was not really doing anything that I would have needed to repent for. Realistically, people sin every day and God knew we would. (Romans 3:23)

For all have sinned and fall short of the
glory of God, (Romans 3:23 NIV)

Well, back to the subject; now that we have some history. I accepted Christ at the age of nineteen. That Sunday, I attended church with my boyfriend and his grandmother. I had never been to that church before, but something stirred within my being that day that I could not shake, tears rolled, and I could not sit still any longer. When they made the alter call, inviting people to accept Christ; I went up. Of all the decisions I have made in life, it has been the absolute best one.

I heard a lot about God and learned to trust Him; sometimes simply because life threw me a hand that was so ridiculous, I could do nothing but rely on Him. Over the years, He has repeatedly shown up in my life; in my mess. God and I became close, and He is working within me, evolving me to becoming who I am, and into who I am also becoming. The person I am becoming is a lady I am proud of and honestly like.

However, the person I am transforming into still has growing to do;

as God is not through with me yet. I have recently turned 52 years old; been married and divorced twice, I had children in and out of wedlock, survived single parenting, operated businesses, been terminated from a job, given a wonderful person to love and lost them, have suffered an injury on the job; which halted my work and my personal business, x-rays that revealed something in my lungs that needed more tests and other personal things going on. I quickly learned that God has me in a growing season; a wilderness. God has thrown me a curve.

In other words, He purposely has me still. As much as I would like to say, I am thrilled because God is elevating me to my next; this has been uncomfortable. I have shed more tears, felt out of control, and tested, Tested, TESTED!!! Evaluated in ways I would have never imagined; and the only thing I know is, that I must trust God through this season; with the understanding that no matter how it turns out, He has my best interest at heart.

It is the feeling of not being in control that stresses me, because it forces me to have to totally take my hands off it and rely completely on God. Yes, why not rely completely on God? Because we are born first into the world only to later realize as Christians, we exist in the world but are not of it. Therefore, we must change our thinking from how it used to be to a stage of trusting and believing in what we cannot see. This is a work in progress for most Christians because faith must be grown.

Even though I had this huge life story of God showing up in my mess, I had become very independent; relying on myself for my bills and things. To be in a position that I could not help myself more was difficult. Not to mention, the business I had fought for; now was standing still with customers on hold. I was a fighter of life, so to be still, not in control and completely rely on God; I just was not ready mind wise. Due to the injury, I could not do things on my own. I had to count on people, and I was not accustomed to that. I was in the middle of redoing my home: decluttering, painting, getting ready to install new floors when I got injured. Therefore, boxes of flooring were sitting in my living room, awaiting installation; as well as other boxes of items that needed to be put in storage or taken to Goodwill. God had me still; still with very little instructions, only a sliver of hope and no idea when this season will end.

To keep from losing my mind, I listened to sermon after sermon, read book after book, studied, and prayed. Prayed and studied, listened to sermon after sermon, sent sermons to other people. I listened to music, prayed more, listened to more sermons, read self-help books, and shed more tears. I cried out to God, "Please help me; this hurts!!!" "I don't know what you're doing, its uncomfortable, really uncomfortable." I cried on my way to work, and then on my way home. I talked to God, I listened for Him to answer and still silence.

Months and months have gone by, and I am still in the wilderness. I started picking up tidbits of information. About the time when I wanted to give up, God gave me a wink. A piece of information, that someone else would not have paid any attention to, was like finding a million dollars to me. Soon the tears slowed, the pain was not as bad, and God was whispering.

Piece by piece, the puzzle is coming together; revealing God's magnificent plan. I am amazed, excited, a little unsure as to where He is taking me. However, during this wilderness I learned; God once again is awesome. I have apologized to him, because there have been moments, I was frustrated and said, "Oh, God got jokes." He will give instructions, have you doing what seems un-logical, and it is all for your good and His glory. It may not seem like it is. It may hurt to no end. I even at one time said," "I know God would not do this to me. Oh, but He did! I never imagined He would give me the love of my life, a great guy and take him away, but it happened.

The thing about God, He will allow things to happen, or He will ordain it. Sounds unjust, but I can promise you, He knows what He is doing. If you hang in there, you will learn valuable things you did not know. God will teach you about yourself. During my season, the prayers grew my faith. Because God sat me down, made me be still, I rested in Him and for myself. Things that I had not done for myself, I was quiet, and had the opportunity to think about them; beginning to put myself first. I also realized how strong of a person I was and that I am immensely proud of who I am, not to mention when evaluated; I shined, my inner light, glowed. (Matthew 5:14)

> *"You are the light of the world. A town built on a hill cannot be hidden. [15] Neither do people light a lamp and put it under a bowl. Instead they put it on its stand, and it gives light to everyone in the house. [16] In the same way, let your light shine before others, that they may see your good deeds and glorify your Father in heaven. (Matthew 5:14-16 NIV)*

During my season, the sermons I shared often blessed other people. In a moment of pain, both physical and mental, I cried half the way to work. At the halfway point, I told God, "I got to get it together." (Clean up my face, hide my tears, make me look like everything is fine, give me strength to get through.) In that moment, I got the push to motivate other people, telling them, there is strength in you, when you can get it together. It was the very first video I ever posted, and it got over five hundred views. I now often post videos, to encourage people and tell them about God. It is always bigger than we think. God is using me, in my mess; to bless others. In fact, looking back, He has been training me for my next season; my entire life.

Because, I was investing time in the word, soon God was revealing things. There were signs and wonders all over the place. The pieces were coming together, and I could see the big picture, as to what God was up to, and now give thanks for this season. I have empathy for anyone that God throws a curve to. All I can say is, "Hold on, keep the faith, trust when you can't see, trust Him scared, trust Him believing and with your unbelief." "Trust Him when it hurts, tell Him it hurts, cry out to Him and never give up." "It is going to be, worth it!"

UNTIL...

OFTEN TRIED TO DECIDE WHERE TO STOP THIS BOOK, AS THERE have been so many moments that God has blessed my life. However, to get this information in your hands, I felt the wilderness season or what I like to call God throwing you a curve was the appropriate time. There will always be moments that God will show up; so, look for a volume two of this book; it is going to be great. What God has done and is doing for me, He can and will do for you if only you believe.

> Then Peter began to speak: "I now realize how true it is that God does not show favoritism. [35] but accepts from every nation the one who fears him and does what is right. (Acts 10: 34-35 NIV)

At this stage in the game, I have successfully raised three beautiful children, they are growing into wonderful men and women of God. I can honestly say, God has covered us, as we have fared better than others in the same situation. I was blessed in writing this and often read the words of my own book; re- living the awesomeness of God. I hope this book will reach every hand that maybe struggling and feeling alone. I pray the words on these pages shows that God does see you and will come to your rescue; that He will encourage you and grow you. Just like God parted the Red Sea for Moses and the children of Israel; He is still doing miracles today.

Years ago, I heard a Motivational Speaker by the name of Dr. Myles Munroe, say, "The only thing that we are given, that is common to everyone is time." "All of us are different heights, different weights, different colors, pigmentation, different economic stature, different ethnic backgrounds, we are *from different cultures, but one thing we all have in common, that's time." "Why is that so important?" "Because what you are and what you become depends on how you use your time." "The billionaire, and the beggar both have 24 hours every day." "We measure life in terms of time." "The old and the young, the black and the white, are all given the same amount of time every day." "Time cannot be stopped." "You cannot stop a day; you cannot stop an hour." "They have no respect for you, but you can control how it will be used." "Which means that even though time is unstoppable it is controllable." "And what you do with it, determines who you become." "Can you honestly say to yourself, that you used time effectively?"*

The only tips I can tell you from my life are: I had faith; sometimes mustard seed, other times "Crazy Faith", and I was never sitting idle. I was trying to help my own self. Faith without works is dead. (James 2:26) I did not send up a prayer and be still, waiting for God to bring my blessing to me; I moved to get it. Praying and waiting does not mean, "Dear God, bless me with a job," but you never apply for it. I sent up a request and started moving in the direction of what I requested.

> *As the body without the spirit is dead, so faith*
> *without deeds is dead. (James 1:26 NIV)*

If you invest in you; work and hustle, life improves. If you sit on the sofa, eating and watching tv; who can we blame for life not progressing? Invest in you, believe in God, and watch Him work!

I must be honest; I had a duh moment while typing the last two chapters; reality set in, that with the exception to a few sections; every portion of this book was a testimony of a blessing God worked in my life. Some were small and others huge, but either way God was moving on my behalf. Therefore, again I say, "I am exceedingly, and abundantly blessed!!!

I know everyone reading this book is not a Christian and that is ok. However, if because of my life's story, you desire to know who God is for yourself and want to be saved; I have listed the Prayer for Salvation below.

Pray this Prayer for Salvation:

Lord, I admit I am a sinner. I need and want your forgiveness. I accept your death as the penalty for my sin and recognize that Your mercy and grace is a gift

You offer to me because of your great love, not based on anything I have done. Cleanse me and make me Your child. By faith I receive You into my heart as the Son of God and as Savior and Lord of my life. From now on, help me live for You, with You in control. In Your precious name, Amen.

> *Jesus answered, "I am the way and the truth and the life. No one comes to the Father except through me. (John 14:6 NIV)*

If you prayed this prayer, CONGRATULATIONS and welcome!!! This will be the greatest decision of your life. At this point, search for a church home so you may grow, and invest in a bible. I recommend New Living Translation because it speaks in the language we speak of today; not thee and thou. Also, look for a bible that introduces the chapter, plus a summary of how the scripture applies to life. This will be valuable to building your faith. God mailed me mine! I was on a book club mailing list; receiving Dr. Suess books and other stories for children when it arrived. I had not requested it; but God knew I would need it and He could not have been more right.

Thank you for reading this book and again, I pray it has blessed you. It is my wish that it has given you hope in a troubled world. I cannot promise you that your days will be easy; as it will not but, I can say with God your outcome is so much better. I urge you to try Him. I genuinely love you and pray for your safety, peace of mind, and abundant blessings to flow your way.

Until next time; be blessed!

REFERENCES

(1996), Daniel A Helminiak. *The Human core of spirituality: mind as psyche and spirit*. August 2 2018. Wikipedia.

"Abundantly Blessed." *I still Believe*. 2010. You tube by Cd Baby.

Bryant, Dr. Jamal. *You;re gonna have to PAY for what you did to ME*. 6 October 2020. You Tube.

Bryne, Rhonda. *The Secret*. Atria Books, 2006.

Devine, Megan. *IT'S OK THAT YOU'RE NOT OK Meeting Grief and Loss in a Culture That Doesn't Understand*. Sounds True, 2017.

Ellen DeGeneres: Relatable. 18 December 2018. Netflix 80166467.

Evans, Tony. *How to Live & Cope with Loss in Your Life*. 23 January 2021. YouTube.

"Faberge Shampoo." *Commercial*. mybeautyads, 29 December 2007.

Furtick, Pastor Steven. *A Lesson in Letting Go*. 26 April 2020. You Tube.

Furtrick, Pastor Steven. *God Can Handle Your Broken Heart*. 1 April 2021. YouTube.

Gray, Dr. John. *Men Are From Mars, Women are from Venus A practical guide for Improving Communication & Getting What You Want in Your Relationships*. Harper Collins, 1992.

Gray, Theodora. "Every day that breath is given, is the opportunity to change, be better, try something new. Don't waste it!" 2007.

—. "If you have a job, you can get a job, if you don't have a job, you can't buy one." n.d.

Groeschel, Pastor Craig. *Thr Faith To Forgive- The Grudge*. 3 November 2019. You Tube.

Henderson, Pastor Keion. *Coping with Collapse*. 20 June 2021. YouTube.

Jakes, TD. *Heart Full of Grief and a Horn Full of Oil*. July 25 2021. YouTube.

—. *Help! I'M RAISING MY CHILDREN ALONE A guide for Single Parents and Those Who Sometime Feel They Are Single*. Charisma House, 2011.

—. *Making Peace With Your Past*. 28 October 2021. You Tube.

—. *Sermon: Bigger Than You Think!* 20 September 2020. You Tube.

—. *Sermon: The Holy Spirit Your CIA Agent Part 1*. 29 September 2013. You tube.

Johnson, Shawn. *When Past Hurts Still Hurt*. 18 July 2021. You Tube.

Jr., Martin Luther King. ""What is Your Lifes Blueprint"." *Part of the King Legacy Series*. Philadelphia: Beacon Press, 26 October 1967. You tube.

Lonergan, Bernard. "The Human Core of Spirituality mind as psyche and spirit." 2 August 2018.

McCarthy, Larry. *Series: Defeating Death*. 12 November 2019. YouTube.

Meyer, Joyce. *How to Forgive and Let Go of your Past*. 15 August 2014. You Tube.

Munroe, Dr. Myles. *Rediscovering the Kingdom vs Redeeming Time.* Shippensburg: Destiny Image Publishers, 2013. paperback.

Nietzsche's, Friedrich. "Maxim and Arrows." *Twilight of the Idols.* 1888. Quora.com.

Osteen, Joel. *Drop It.* 11 January 2016. You Tube.

Press, Oxford University. *Definition of Fear with Synomyms and Antonyms.* 2023. Oxford Language.

Speaks, Stephen. *5 Reasons Why God Will Send You The RIGHT MAN At the Wrong Time.* 18 March 2022. You Tube.

Stanley, Dr. Charles. *The Courage to Keep Going.* 20 November 2022. YouTube.

The Holy Bible King James Version. One Million Words, n.d.

The Holy Bible, New International Version. Zondervan, 2011.

The Philip Lief Group. *Roget's 21st Century Thesaurus Third Edition.* n.d. Thesaurus.com.

Todd, Michael. *Be Careful What You're Anchored To.* 2023 21 February. You Tube.

—. *CRAZY FAITH: It's only Crazy Until it Happens.* WaterBrook, 2021.

unknown. *Crosswalk.* 6 August 202. 22 December 2022.

Warren, Rick. *The Purpose Driven Life.* Zondervan, 2002.

Wilson, Dr. Sandy. *Hope and Healing for Yourself and your Relatioships Hurt People Hurt People.* Our Daily Bread Publishing, 2015.

Ziglar, Zig. "How to Create Your Own Future and Get What You Want Motivation." @justwatch7033, 19 Sep 2017.

ABOUT THE AUTHOR

Theodora Gray is an extraordinary person. One encounter with her and you'll never be the same. Her smile is infectious, and her warm bubbly personality lights up any room. She is your cheerleader and biggest fan; who gives pep talks, motivates, and encourages you; as easy as breathing. It her deep desire to make a difference by allowing God to use her. The love she has for him is never hidden. Theodora has over thirty years of experience, witnessing the many moments God has come to her rescue; by building the business, helping with parenting, or surviving the bad relationship. Theodora credits God with her ability to write, and often allows him to speak to her, or through her with the flow of a pen. It is her wish with this book; to magnify God's name and give hope in a world that is increasingly growing out of control. Theodora Gray lives in Vermont, with her three children and two dogs.